THE PHENOMENON OF RELIGION

Pagan and Biblical Religion

Some Reflections on the Bifurcation of the
Religious Phenomenon between the Dimension-of-Power
and the Dimension-of-Consciousness

Manfred H. Vogel

University Press of America,® Inc.
Lanham · Boulder · New York · Toronto · Plymouth, UK

Copyright © 2007 by
University Press of America,® Inc.
4501 Forbes Boulevard
Suite 200
Lanham, Maryland 20706
UPA Acquisitions Department (301) 459-3366

Estover Road
Plymouth PL6 7PY
United Kingdom

All rights reserved

British Library Cataloging in Publication Information Available

Library of Congress Control Number: 2006937937
ISBN-13: 978-0-7618-3664-3 (paperback :   paper)
ISBN-10: 0-7618-3664-0 (paperback :   paper)

Dedicated to my grandchildren—Jordan, Aaron, Benjamin, Rachel, Sofie, Lucas, and Josephine.

Contents

I.	Delineating the Religious Phenomenon	1
II.	Paganism and the Hebrew Bible	15
III.	Halachic Judaism, Christianity and Islam—The Three "Daughter Religions" of the Hebrew Bible	49
IV.	The Religious Phenomenon in the Context of the Modern World	87
	About the Author	97

I

Delineating the Religious Phenomenon

Among the various delineations of the phenomenon of religion that have been put forth we find the delineation associated with the Protestant theologian/philosopher of religion Paul Tillich to be the most persuasive. According to this delineation, religion comes to address, i.e., to overcome, what is being perceived as a predicament characterizing human existence and, indeed, not just any run-of-the-mill predicament but a predicament that is ultimate, the ultimate predicament in the sense of being the most fundamental and essential predicament characterizing human existence.[1] Namely, religion comes to offer a "cure" (or extend assistance in attaining a "cure") to what is being "diagnosed" as the ultimate predicament characterizing human existence.[2]

The justification for our saying that we find Tillich's delineation most persuasive rests on the fact that it meets most fully and clearly the three conditions that, in our view, any valid delineation of the religious phenomenon must satisfy. Thus, it meets the condition that the religious phenomenon must formulate itself specifically and exclusively with respect to the human situation. For clearly, the phenomenon can be encountered only with respect to the human entity and not with respect to any other entity—animals don't have religion and, as we shall presently see in conjunction with the second condition, neither do angels. Indeed, not only can the religious phenomenon be encountered only with respect to the human entity but it is encountered with respect to the human entity at all places and at all times wherever the human entity can be found from the moment it emerges in the evolutionary process (and this being the case, it should not be surprising that this condition, in contradistinction to the other two conditions, is met by practically all the many various delineations of the religious phenomenon that have been put forth.) Secondly, it meets the condition that not only does the delineation of the religious phenomenon have to formulate itself with respect to the human situation but that it must address itself specifically to the fundamental predicament that has been identified within the human situation. If such focusing on the ultimate predicament is absent because no such problematic has been identified in the human situation or because the delineation fails to direct itself to the predicament, the delineation could not be valid. For without the recognition of the existence of a fundamental predicament within the human situation the very rationale for the religious phenomenon to arise is taken away—angels have no need for religion, nor does the human who would live in the Garden of Eden. Thirdly, it meets the condition that not only must the religious phenomenon be delineated as addressing the human situation and focusing clearly on the fundamental predicament that it presents, but it must also be delineated as being, in its very essence, constituted as an enterprise that is involved in fundamentally transforming the human situation in that it not only recognizes the fundamental predicament that it contains but in that it offers a way of overcoming it. The religious enterprise is, so to speak, in the business of offering salvation/redemption—without it, it loses its *raison d'être* (indeed, it becomes a metaphysical rather than a religious enterprise). And this of course means that a valid delineation of the religious phenomenon would have to place the phenomenon principally within the arena of praxis rather than in the arena of theory, seeing that the phenomenon must necessarily implicate action rather than mere description. (Indeed inasmuch as the religious phenomenon formulates itself in terms of a "cure" rather than of a "diagnosis," it must inescapably implicate acting rather than description.)[3] Of course, the phenomenon though placed within the arena of praxis would inescapably implicate, in turn, a *Weltanschauung* as the required context in which it can arise and function and such implication could be encompassed only within the arena of theory.

But now clearly, inasmuch as we are dealing here with a predicament that is ultimate, the predicament cannot be transitory or contingent. It must be a permanent and unchanging fixture as regards its bearer. And this being the case, it must mean, of course, that the predicament here must ground itself in an aspect of the human situation that is itself permanent and unchangeable. The one and only such aspect that can meet this requirement, i.e., the requirement that it be permanent and unchanging, is, we would submit, the ontological constitution of the human.[4] Thus, for the ultimate predicament to be authentically ultimate it must ground itself in some feature of the ontological constitution of the human entity and this, in turn, must mean that the ultimate predicament has to formulate itself here in the context of the dimension in which the ontological constitution of the human constitutes itself.

The human entity, however, constitutes itself ontologically, we would submit, not in the context of a single dimension but in the context of two mutually irreducible dimensions (as such, the human entity is indeed unique, seeing that all other possible entities, either in the realm of nature or in the realm of the divine, constitute themselves ontologically in the context of a single dimension). Thus, one of the two dimensions manifests itself in the physical body possessed by the human entity while the other dimension manifests itself in the states of awareness experienced by the human entity, for example, awareness of sense-perception, of thinking, of volition or of feeling. And this being the case, we propose to refer to the first dimension as the dimension-of-power and to the second dimension as the dimension-of-consciousness, seeing that in our judgment a persuasive case can be made that the ultimate, so to speak, "stuff" or "element" in terms of which the dimension manifesting itself in material/physical entities constitutes itself is energy, i.e., power, and that the ultimate "stuff" or "element" in terms of which the dimension manifesting itself in the experiences of awareness constitutes itself is consciousness (which, in turn, expresses itself most penetratingly when manifesting itself as self-consciousness). Alternatively, we may also use Buberian terminology and interchangeably refer to these two dimensions respectively as the It-dimension and the Thou-dimension. We can make this identification between the dimension-of-power and the It-dimension on the one hand and the dimension-of consciousness and the Thou-dimension on the other hand because we would want to claim that a good case can be made that Buber's bifurcation between the It and the Thou can be reduced ultimately to the bifurcation between power and consciousness respectively.[5]

Apprehending reality in terms of such a bifurcation goes back to earliest times in human history and was very widely, one is tempted to say universally, accepted, though it did not express itself in terms of power versus consciousness, but instead in such terms as matter versus spirit, flesh versus soul, body versus mind, this-worldliness versus other-worldliness (the first terms in these bifurcations reflecting the dimension-of-power while the second terms reflecting the dimension-of-consciousness). True, in recent times the tendency among many distinguished scientists and philosophers has been to claim that the phenomenon of consciousness will be shown, if not already then in the not too distant future, to be fully reducible to some neural activity. And inasmuch as neural activity is fully reducible to electrical or chemical transactions and these transactions, in turn, are, in the last analysis, but transactions in terms of power (i.e., energy), the clear implication of the claim here is that the dualistic view whereby reality in its ontological constitution bifurcates itself between power and consciousness is, in the last analysis, reducible to a monistic view whereby reality is being ontologically constituted exclusively in terms of power.

Indeed, it must be conceded that this claim is supported by some very persuasive considerations. Thus, for example, the most telling consideration is the undeniable fact that for the phenomenon of consciousness to manifest itself (in the act of thinking, willing, or feeling) the presence of a neurological mechanism, i.e., a brain which is a physical entity constituted by power, is a condition *sine qua non* which, in turn, would implicate that consciousness is depended on power—no brain, no consciousness (and even more remarkable, it has been established that certain specific manifestations of consciousness are dependent on the functioning of certain specific parts of the brain). But as has been noted by some philosophers dealing with the issue of consciousness, the dependency of consciousness on the availability of the brain is established with respect to its manifestation as it impinges on us (given the ontological constitution of the human, consciousness can arise for it only through the mediation of the brain) but it is not established with respect to how consciousness in its own terms arises. And here lies the rub, as far as we are concerned. For we cannot for the life of use comprehend how a circuit of electrical/chemical transactions, no matter how quantitatively complicated it be, could produce an act of awareness. There seems to be an unbridgeable gap between neural activity and an act of consciousness—the two are qualitatively different. But even if we grant the possibility that electrical/chemical transactions can produce acts of consciousness, thus reducing the genesis of consciousness to the activity of power, a case can be made that this would not undermine our contention that the ontological constitution of reality is to be seen as being bifurcated between the dimension-of-power and the dimension-of-consciousness. For regardless how consciousness comes into being (whether as the result of neural activity or independently of it), once its being is established it clearly manifests characterizations that are fundamentally distinct from (indeed, in many cases diametrically opposed to) those manifested by power, and this clearly has a direct and fundamental bearing on our undertaking here, namely, on our attempt to delineate the meaning and the significance of the religious phenomenon.

Now, given the context of a reality that is bifurcated between a dimension-of-power and a dimension-of-consciousness, we can, at least theoretically speaking, have more than one kind of the religious phenomenon and correspondingly of the divine entity, seeing that their nature is directly determined by the "stuff" constituting the dimension in which they are formulated. Thus, with respect to the notion of the divine entity, the number of possible different kinds of divine entities that theoretically we can have is to be exactly the same as the number of different dimensions implicated in the reality with which we are concerned. Indeed, as already noted, the essential signification of the notion of divinity is ultimacy, namely, a divine entity is an entity that expresses in an ultimate manner the "stuff" in terms of which the dimension in which it is implicated constitutes itself. As such, there has to be indeed an exact numerical correspondence between the number of the different dimensions involved and the number of the different divine entities implicated. And inasmuch as in our context we have two dimensions involved, the dimension-of-power and the dimension-of-consciousness (this context, by the way, being uniquely relevant to the human entity, seeing that only the human entity ontologically constitutes itself in terms of two dimensions), we can theoretically have two kinds of divine entities—a divine entity that is ultimate in terms of power and a divine entity that is ultimate in terms of consciousness, in other words an It-god and a Thou-god.[6]

When we move, however from the question of how many different kinds of divine entities can theoretically be available to how many different types of religious phenomena can theoretically be available, the one-to-one correspondence that was obtained between the number of different kinds of divine entities that theoretically can be functioning and the number of different dimensions that are present breaks down. For, given our delineation of the religious phenomenon, the number of the different types of the religious phenomenon that could theoretically be available will be determined, in the last analysis, by how many different ultimate predicaments could be "diagnosed" with respect to the number of dimensions involved. And here, in principle, we would always be provided with a greater number of different types of the religious phenomenon than the number of different kinds of dimensions that are involved. Specifically, in our case where we have two different kinds of dimension involved, i.e., the dimension-of-power (or the It-dimension) and the dimension-of-consciousness (or the Thou-dimension), we can theoretically come up with five different kinds of ultimate predicaments and therefore with five different types of the religious phenomenon.

Thus, we can have an ultimate predicament and correspondingly a religious phenomenon that formulate themselves exclusively in terms of the dimension-of-power (we would submit that the ultimate predicament here would express itself in terms of finitude). Secondly, we can have an ultimate predicament and a religious phenomenon that formulate themselves exclusively in terms of the dimension-of-consciousness (and here, we would submit, the ultimate predicament formulates itself in terms of aloneness). Thirdly, we can also have (albeit only with respect to the human entity, seeing that only the human entity constitutes itself in terms of both dimensions) an ultimate predicament and commensurately a religious phenomenon that formulate themselves neither exclusively in terms of the dimension-of-power nor exclusively in terms of the dimension-of-consciousness but in terms of both dimensions, namely, in terms of the relative balance, i.e., the relative weight and dominance allotted to each dimension, that ought to obtain between the two dimensions. But as such, this third theoretically possible formulation breaks itself up into three different formulations so that we really have not one but three additional formulations. Namely we can theoretically have a formulation that basically reflects the state of affairs in the foregoing overall formulation in which the ultimate predicament is constituted by the balance between the two dimensions being askew (while in theory it can be askew either in favor of the dimension-of-power or in favor of the dimension-of-consciousness, in actuality we can encounter the former but not the latter) and in which, therefore, the "solution" offered by the religious phenomenon would consist in setting the balance aright. But now in addition we can have two further formulations at two diametrically opposite poles in which the ultimate predicament and hence the "solution" offered by the religious phenomenon are formulated in maximal terms. Thus, we can theoretically have a formulation in which the very presence of the dimension-of-power within the ontological constitution of the human entity constitutes the ultimate predicament and in which, therefore, the "solution" offered by the religious phenomenon would consist in the eradication of the dimension-of-power from the ontological constitution of the human entity. And secondly, we can theoretically also have a formulation that is a mirror image of the foregoing formulation, namely, a formulation in which the very presence of the dimension-of-consciousness within the ontological constitution of the human entity constitutes the ultimate predicament and in which, therefore, the "solution" offered by the religious phenomenon would consist in the eradication of the dimension-of-consciousness from the ontological constitution of the human entity.

Now we would want to claim that these various formulations presented here, namely, the two formulations regarding the kind of divine entity and the five formulations regarding the type of religion, are, by and large, not merely products of hypothetical speculative theorizing but formulations that find expression in the actual concrete history of the religious phenomenon. We qualify our claim by the "by and large" because we have to concede that with regard to the formulations concerning the type of religion, the claim, as far as we can see, could not be substantiated with respect to the second alternative in the third formulation and may not be substantiated with the degree of clarity and certainty that one would have liked with respect to the third alternative in the third formulation. But with respect to all the other formulations, we believe that it can be shown that the claim can be fully substantiated. Of course, to do this we must turn to examine the expressions of various concrete, historical religions. It is to this task that the remainder of this essay is devoted.

Notes

1. By the way, the delineation here is also formulated in terms of an ultimate concern rather than in terms of an ultimate predicament. It would seem to us, however, that although there is no contradiction or inconsistency between these two ways of delineating the phenomenon of religion, there is, nonetheless, an important difference between the two delineations (which, in particular, impinges upon our concern here, namely the concern to establish the fundamental state of affairs in which the phenomenon of religion grounds itself) and in which the delineation in terms of an ultimate predicament has a significant advantage over the delineation in terms of an ultimate concern. This advantage can be seen with respect to two considerations. First, the delineation in terms of an ultimate predicament grounds the religious phenomenon in the objective realm (e.g., in the finitude of the human entity or in the absence of justice, righteousness, in the collective life of mankind) while the delineation in terms of an ultimate concern grounds the religious phenomenon in the subjective realm (i.e., in the human emotional response to what is perceived to be the ultimate predicament). Secondly, the delineation in terms of an ultimate predicament grounds the religious phenomenon in a more fundamental, primary manner. For while it is true that in a sense both delineations implicate each other, the delineation in terms of an ultimate concern is implicated by the delineation in terms of an ultimate predicament as its consequence while the delineation in terms of an ultimate predicament is implicated by the delineation in terms of an ultimate concern as its cause. Because of these considerations we prefer the delineation of the religious phenomenon that is in terms of an ultimate predicament though clearly the delineation in terms of an ultimate concern is equally valid, seeing that it is fully consistent with, and indeed entailed by, the delineation in terms of an ultimate predicament.

2. Here too, Tillich's delineation lends itself to two different readings. According to one reading (this reading being linked to the version whereby the religious phenomenon is delineated in terms of an ultimate concern rather than in terms of an ultimate predicament, i.e., the object of the religious phenomenon being the ultimate concern rather than the ultimate predicament of the human entity), the "diagnosis" can be established either

through the enterprise of philosophy, i.e., the philosophy of religion, or through the enterprise of religion itself, i.e., theology, with the advantage, however, being given to the latter over the former on the grounds that while the former establishes the "diagnosis" exclusively from the human perspective, the latter adds a transcendental perspective to its human perspective. True, in a sense, both the religious and the philosophic enterprise implicate both the "diagnosis" and the "cure," seeing that each implicates the other. But we would submit that while in the religious enterprise the "diagnosis" is implicated by the "cure," in the philosophic enterprise, the "cure" is implicated by the "diagnosis," for in the religious enterprise the primary concern is with the "cure" while in the philosophic enterprise it is with the "diagnosis." As such, a "division of labor" between the two enterprises does obtain and therefore the second reading which does introduce such a "division of labor" between the religious and the philosophic enterprises is, in our judgment, more applicable.

3. By the way, as one could have readily inferred from the observation made above in reference to the first condition, there are many delineations of the religious phenomenon that fail to meet these latter conditions, i.e., the second and the third conditions. To bring only two examples, let us first cite the very widely known and influential delineation by Rudolph Otto whereby the religious phenomenon constitutes itself in terms of a *suis generic* human experience, i.e., the experience of the numinous, which, in turn, elicits from the human the dual and contradictory responses of dread and fascination. And secondly one can cite Abraham Joshua Heschel's delineation whereby the religious phenomenon constitutes itself as the human response to the profound mystery presented to it by the world it encounters, a response that expresses itself in terms of awe, amazement and wonder (though to Heschel's credit, it must be stated that he recognizes that the mystery eliciting the feelings of awe, amazement and wonder is not the ultimate, the final word, within the context of the religious phenomenon—the ultimate is the meaning that lies beyond the mystery). Clearly, in both of these instances the religious phenomenon is constituted in terms of a description of unchanging human experiences which in no way implicates any activity that may impinge on the given affairs in order to transform them.

4. Of course, even the ontological constitution of the human is not permanent and unchanging if these are to be taken in an absolutist sense. For given enough time, the ontological constitution of the human may well evolve into a different ontological constitution. True, but then we would no longer be dealing with the human entity but with another kind of entity. And since, as we have seen, the religious phenomenon is linked exclusively with the human entity, it may well disappear with the disappearance of the human entity. Thus, for all intents and purposes, the ontological constitution of the human entity can be legitimately taken as providing the religious phenomenon with a permanent and unchanging aspect which as such can safeguard the ultimacy of the predicament implicated in it.

5. True, Buber applies the bifurcation between the It and the Thou primarily with respect to the realm of relations (namely, he divides all possible relations between the I-It and the I-Thou kind of relation) and not with respect to individual entities or particular dimensions. But clearly, a case can be made that relations necessarily implicate entities, seeing that a relation must be bounded on either one of its two sides thus implicating two entities as the poles bounding the relation and as such sharing fully in the characterization attributed to the relation (indeed, Buber's naming of the two kinds of relation as the I-It and the I-Thou would be more precisely named as the It-It and the Thou-Thou kinds of relation respectively). And this being the case, it should not be surprising, after all, to find Buber in certain instances characterizing entities taken in themselves, i.e., in isolation from the relation in which they may be implicated, as It or Thou entities as, for example,

when he introduces the distinction between an It-god and a Thou-god (the It-god being exemplified by the "god of the philosophers" and the Thou-god being exemplified by the "god of Abraham, Isaac and Jacob"). Similarly, a case can be made that the ontological constitution of an entity necessarily implicates an ontological dimension, to wit, the ontological dimension in terms of which the entity constitutes itself ontologically. Thus, although in this case Buber himself does not seem to extend his It-Thou bifurcation to the realm of dimensions, such an extension is clearly not only feasible but is necessarily implicated by the It-Thou bifurcation that has been established in the preceding instance with respect to the realm of entities—the It-Thou bifurcation established by Buber with respect to the realm of relations in necessarily implicating itself in the realm of entities also necessarily implicates itself in the realm of dimensions, giving us It and Thou entities and an It and a Thou dimension.

Now we would submit that an identification between an It-dimension and a dimension-of-power, on the one hand, and a Thou-dimension and a dimension-of-consciousness, on the other, can be established. True, as already noted, Buber himself does not provide us with such an identification, focusing instead his attention exclusively on describing the various aspects that characterize the two kinds of relation which he has noted and to which he refers respectively as the I-It and the I-Thou kind of relation (the reference here stemming from one of the aspects in terms of which the bifurcation within the realms of relations is precipitated, namely, the aspect of whether, grammatically speaking, the object in the relation restricts itself to the second person or whether it allows itself to be extended to the third person). Thus, for example, the I-It relation is characterized by him as a relation of utilization; as a one-way relation from a grammatical subject to a grammatical object; as a relation in which the grammatical object is related to as a means to a further end, itself being passive, on the receiving end of the action emanating from the grammatical subject (thus a relation in which the subject-object distinction signifies not only a grammatical but also, more fundamentally, an ontological differentiation); as a relation which lends itself to being descriptive of its grammatical object (thus of relating to it in the third person, as an It); and lastly, as a relation which is, ontologically speaking, secondary and external to the entities constituting its grammatical subject and object. As against this, the I-Thou relation is characterized as a relation of address which as such implicates itself as a relation of affirmation; as a relation in which the grammatical object is related to as an end-in-itself and as such is being constituted as an ontological subject; as a relation of authentic mutuality, i.e., a relation where the mutuality is constituted by the relation oscillating between the two ontological subjects (and not by the overlapping of two one-way relations moving simultaneously in opposite directions); and lastly, as a relation that is, ontologically speaking, primary to and internal with respect to the two entities, i.e., the two ontological subjects, which it relates (the two entities arising by virtue of their being the two poles delimiting the relation on both of its two sides thus constituting themselves in terms of the relation which as such implicates the relation as ontologically primary and their own ontological constitution as being, by its very essence, relational).

We would submit, however, that the defining characterization of the I-It and the I-Thou relations respectively (defining in the sense that they implicate the other characterizations attributed by Buber to the relation) is the characterization of the I-It relation as a relation of utilization and of the I-Thou relation as a relation of affirmation, namely, that the I-It relation is, by its very essence, a relation of utilization and thus that all its other characterizations receive their rationale, their validity, from its being a relation of utilization and likewise that the I-Thou relation is, by its very essence, a relation of affirmation and thus that all its other characterizations receive their rationale, their validity, from its being a relation of affirmation. Thus, the I-It relation in being, by its very essence, a relation of utilization necessarily implicates that it can only be a one-way relation, seeing that it can move only in one direction from the entity that is the utilizer to the entity that is being utilized; at the same time it also necessarily implicates that the grammatical object in the relation, i.e., the entity that is being utilized, can only be related to as a means to a further end desired by the entity that is the utilizer for, after all, this is what utilization means—using an other as a means to some desired end; furthermore, it also implicates its availability to being descriptive, seeing that utilization necessarily implicates that the agent, i.e., the entity which is the utilizer, be oriented with regard to the various entities present within the parameters of its experiential world which, in turn, implicates that a description of this world be available (which, in its turn, implicates that the capacity to abstract and thus impose duration, i.e., a measure of permanence, on the entities existing within the flux of the experiential world be also available); lastly, it implicates that the status of the relation involved in the act of utilization is, ontologically speaking, secondary and external to the entities involved in the act, seeing that without a preceding existence of an entity that has the capacity and drive to utilize and the preceding existence of an entity which in relation to the former entity lends itself to being utilized, a relation of utilization would not arise while the entities involved in the relation here can clearly come into existence and sustain themselves in isolation, i.e., apart from being involved in any relation of utilization—the relation here does not constitute a necessary and internal ingredient in the ontological structure of the entities and as such is devoid of ontological priority with respect to them. Likewise, the I-Thou relation in being, by its very essence, a relation of affirmation necessarily implicates that it can arise only when it relates to the other as an end-in-itself, for after all this is what, in the last analysis, affirmation means—establishing and thus accepting the other as an end-in-itself (and as such, indeed, being able to express itself only in the form of address); this clearly means that it is a relation between two ontological subjects which, in turn, implicates that the relation here must be a relation of authentic mutuality and as such excluding the possibility of its lending itself to being descriptive (seeing that this would necessarily implicate that the other, i.e., the grammatical object, here must be an entity constituting itself as an ontological object which would clearly contradict the claim that the relation here is a relation between two ontological subjects); and lastly, seeing that the relation here must be a relation of authentic mutuality implicates that the relation here is, ontologically speaking, prior to the entities it relates and that it is thus inherent in their very ontological constitution.

But if this be the case, namely, that the defining aspect (in the sense that all other aspects are deducible from it) of the I-It relation is that it is a relation of utilization and that the defining aspect of the I-Thou relation is that it is a relation of affirmation, then a good case can be made that all I-It relations must ground themselves in the dimension-of-power and that all I-Thou relations must ground themselves in the dimension-of-consciousness (and that, indeed, both kinds of relation ground themselves not only in terms of a single characterization, i.e., in terms of the characterization of utilization in the I-It relation and the characterization of affirmation in the I-Thou relation, but in terms of the sum total of all their characterizations, seeing that all these characterizations are, as already noted, deducible from and thus reducible to the characterizations of utilization and affirmation respectively). For a relation of utilization can arise, i.e., can constitute itself, only in the context of the dimension-of-power and a relation of affirmation can arise only in the context of the dimension-of-consciousness. Utilization can arise only if the relating to an other is in terms of power and conversely any relating to an other that is in the form of utilization inescapably presupposes that the relating is in terms of power; likewise, affirmation can make sense only if the one who affirms and the one to whom the affirmation is directed possess consciousness and conversely consciousness (or, more precisely, self-consciousness) can come into existence and sustain itself in it only by being related to in terms of affirmation.

The grounding of the Buberian It/Thou bifurcation within the contexts of the dimension-of-power and the dimension-of-consciousness respectively which is being pursued here is not, however, limited to the realm of the relation, i.e., to the I-It and the I-Thou relations, but is extendable to the realm of the entity, i.e., to the It-entities and the Thou-entities. For, as has been noted above, the characterization of the relation would also apply to the entities implicated in the relation. As such, inasmuch as the It and Thou entities come to possess the characterizations of the I-It and the I-Thou relations respectively and inasmuch as these characterizations ground themselves in the dimension-of-power and the dimension-of-consciousness respectively, these characterizations cause not only the I-It and the I-Thou relations but also the It and Thou entities to ground themselves in the dimension-of-power and the dimension-of-consciousness respectively. Lastly, inasmuch as the grounding within the dimension-of-power and the dimension-of-consciousness respectively encompasses all the I-It relations and all the It entities in the former and all the I-Thou relations and all the Thou entities in the latter, an identity between the It-dimension and the dimension-of-power, on the one hand, and between the Thou-dimension and the dimension-of-consciousness, on the other, can be readily established. For the characterization of a dimension and thus its constitution is nothing else but the characterization manifested by the kind of relations and thus of entities which it encompasses. As such, we can say that the sum total of a certain kind of relations and thus of a certain kind of entities encompassed within a particular dimension constitute the content of that dimension and determine the parameters of its signification; in other words, we can say that there is an identity between the sum total of a certain kind of relations and entities, on the one hand, and a particular dimension on the other hand. In our case here this means that there is an identity between the sum total of the I-It relations and the It entities, on the one hand, and the It-dimension on the other hand, and similarly between the sum total of the I-Thou relations and the Thou entities, on the one hand, and the Thou-dimension, on the other hand. And this, in turn, means that by establishing above that I-It relations and It entities ground themselves in the dimension-of-power and that I-Thou relations and Thou entities ground themselves in the dimension-of-consciousness, we have also established that the It-dimension grounds itself in and thus, for all intents and purposes, is identical with the dimension-of-power and similarly that the Thou-dimension grounds itself in and thus, for all intents and purposes, is identical with the dimension-of-consciousness. And this being the case, the Buberian terminology of It versus Thou and the terminology of power versus consciousness can indeed be used interchangeably.

One further comment, stated very briefly, may be in order here. Namely, in establishing an identity between the It-dimension and the dimension-of-power, on the one hand, and between the Thou-dimension and the dimension-of-consciousness, on the other hand, we are provided with much more than merely two nomenclatures that are interchangeable. We are provided with a rationale for the respective characterizations ascribed by Buber to his I-It and I-Thou relations respectively. For as already noted, while Buber gives us a very insightful description of the various characterizations he ascribes to his I-It and the I-Thou relations (and in consequence of this to his It and Thou entities) respectively, and, even more perceptively, dividing their ascription between the two kinds of relation (and the two kinds of entity), he does not give us any rationale for these various characterizations and for their ascription to one or the other of the two kinds of relation (and of entity). As he says, he merely goes to the window and points out to us what he

Delineating the Religious Phenomenon

sees outside. Still, the question by virtue of what does a relation or its corresponding entities assume the characterizations that Buber observes in them forces itself upon us. Clearly, referring to a relation or to its corresponding entities in terms of It or Thou gives us no clue as to the answer. The terms It and Though merely designate two kinds of relation—the numbers 1 and 2 or the letters a and b would have done just as well (true, they are chosen by Buber because they reflect the two aspects of one particular characterization deemed by him to be more readily available to our observation, these two aspects being that in one kind of relation the grammatical object can be in the third person singular, i.e., an it, while in the other kind of relation the grammatical object can only be in the second person singular, i.e., a you; but this in no way changes the fact that the terms It and Thou merely designate and do not provide us with a rationale). It is quite a different matter, however, when one shifts from the terms It and Thou to the notions of power and consciousness respectively, namely, when one identifies the term It with the notion of power and the term Thou with the notion of consciousness. For now it can be shown that all the characterizations ascribed to the It-dimension (in its expression either in the realm of the relation, i.e., in the I-It relation, or in the realm of the entity, i.e., the It entity) are implicated in the notion of power and likewise that all the characterizations ascribed to the Thou-dimension (again, in its expression either in the realm of relation, i.e., in the I-Thou relation or in the realm of the entity, i.e., the Thou entity) are implicated in the notion of consciousness.

Thus, we would submit that the various characterizations ascribed to the It-dimension as for example 1) that the reality constituting itself in its context constitutes itself as an unbroken continuum (and thus presenting us with a monistic or, to use theological terminology, a pantheistic view of itself); 2) that it lends itself to gradation which, in turn, means that it lend itself to being quanticized; 3) that space and time can be constituted solely within its context, serving as the framework in which all its expressions/manifestations have to locate themselves; 4) that the category of the entity is the primary ontological category here while the category of the relation is a secondary category being contingent on that of the entity; 5) that all the entities here are embedded in an unbroken, continuous flux and where, therefore, any degree of permanence (which only as such would allow the feasibility of their being described and thus affording us the possibility of orienting ourselves with respect to them) can be attained only by abstracting them from their concrete existence; and 6) that the only kind of relation that can arise within the context of the It-dimension is a relation of utilization (which as such implicates, in turn, that it can only be a one-way relation and a relation in which the other, i.e., the grammatical object in the relation, can only be related to as a means to a further end)—that all these characterizations can be provided with a persuasive rationale only by identifying the It-dimension with the dimension-of-power, which is to say, only on the basis that the It-dimension constitutes itself in terms of power. For power (i.e., energy, force), by its very essence, constitutes itself in terms of motion (indeed, it is nothing else but motion) and the progression of motion is an uninterrupted continuum excluding any possibility of a "jump" over a "gap" or of a "rest" in the progression, thus accounting for the first and the fifth characterizations). Further, motion with respect to its speed lends itself to gradation and thus to being quanticized—it can move faster and slower and as such manifest more and less power, thus accounting for the second characterization. Moreover, in principle, there is no limit to the speed that motion can attain. Not only that, but by its very nature motion (and thus power) is always striving to increase its speed and as such is "imperialistic," thus accounting for the sixth characterization, seeing that utilization is but the way by which the "imperialistic" tendency brings about its actualization. (By the way, a limit is placed on the acceleration of the speed of the motion—or on the increase in its power—by the fact that motion can, and in fact always does, progress simultaneously in two opposite directions, forward and backward, so that the speed in the direction where it is greater is reduced by the speed in the opposite direction, the latter acting as the "breaks" limiting the acceleration of the former. Indeed, when the speed of the motion is reduced sufficiently so that it falls within the parameters delineating the range of our sense-perception, the power involved manifests itself—or, put alternatively, the motion involved "embodies" itself—as a concrete entity which as such makes it the primary ontological category with respect to our experiential world while the relation, arising as it does by the impingement of one concrete entity on another concrete entity, is clearly an ontological category here only secondarily, thus accounting for the fourth characterization). Lastly, both space and time are by their very essence inextricably linked to the progression of motion, seeing that their very constitution is brought about by it. If there were no motion, neither space nor time could have arisen to underlie our experiential world by serving as the framework in which all its manifestations must locate themselves, thus accounting for the third characterization.

Likewise, we would also submit that the various characterizations ascribed to the Thou-dimension as for example 1) that the reality constituting itself in its context constitutes itself as a bifurcated reality, bifurcated between the subject and its object, between the self and the other, a reality that constitutes itself in terms of over-againstness, i.e., in terms of unbridgeable "gaps" between its constituent entities; 2) that it does not lend itself to gradation and thus to being quanticized; 3) that it expresses itself outside space and time; 4) that its primary ontological expression is in terms of the category of the relation, the category of the entity being a secondary ontological expression; 5) that the only kind of relation that can arise in its context is a relation of affirmation, a relation which implicates that the other is to be related to only as an end-in-itself (and not as a means to some further end) and which as such further implicates that the other can only be addressed (and not described); and 6) that the relation that arises in its context is a relation of authentic mutuality (and not a one-way relation nor, for that matter, an overlap of two one-way relations moving simultaneously in opposite directions)—that all these characterizations can be provided with a persuasive rationale only by identifying the Thou-dimension with the dimension-of-consciousness, which is to say, only on the basis that the Thou-dimension constitutes itself in terms of consciousness. For in contradistinction to power, consciousness in no way implicates motion (it implicates a presence that is eternal in the sense of subsisting outside the progression of time from a past to a future, thus a presence that subsists in an eternal present), and consequently space and time cannot constitute themselves in its context nor can it lend itself to gradation and therefore to being quanticized (the act of consciousness when taken in its own terms and not in terms of its "refraction" within the dimension-of-power is all or none), thus accounting for the second and third characterizations. At the same time, in being, by its very essence, constituted as a "consciousness of" something or someone, the primary ontological expression of consciousness is in terms of the category of the relation (the category of the entity arising secondarily as the pole of the relation) and this, in turn, implicates a reality that excludes the possibility of its being constituted as a continuum (or, to use Levinas' terminology, that excludes the possibility of its being ascribed the notions of totality and sameness), thus accounting for the first and fourth characterizations. Lastly a case can be made that for an entity that is the bearer of consciousness or, more precisely, for an entity that is the bearer of self-consciousness, to come into existence and sustain itself in it, an affirmation extended by another from the outside would be required and that the mechanism by which such an affirmation would be effected is by the entity extending its affirmation to that other who by acknowledging the affirmation extends its affirmation to it, both the extending and the acknowledging taking place, however, simultaneously in one act thus accounting for the fifth and sixth characterizations.

6. This is so inasmuch as the divine entity as formulated here reflects in its ontological constitution the ontological constitution of the dimension that implicates it and as such it can very conveniently serve us as a very good indicator of what kind of dimension provides the context here—knowing the kind of divine entity would at the same time establish for us the kind of dimension with which we are dealing. But useful as this function may be for us, it should be noted that it is not the real function of the divine entity. Its real function is to be seen not in the role it plays with respect to our convenience but rather in the role it plays within the very context of the religious phenomenon itself. And here the essential function of the divine entity is constituted by the role it plays in connection with the salvific/redemptive aspect of the phenomenon, namely, with the aspect of overcoming the fundamental predicament rather than with the aspect of "diagnosing" it. There are in the main two roles that the divine entity can play here. On the one hand it can provide itself as the model of the entity that is fully realized within the salvific/redemptive state of existence, i.e., as the model of the entity that has fully overcome the fundamental predicament, while, on the other hand it can provide itself as an active agent inextricably implicated in the bringing about of the salvific/redemptive state of existence, i.e., as an active agent in the overcoming of the fundamental predicament.

Indeed, we would submit that within the dimension-of-power the divine entity is likely to function primarily as a model and not as an active agent. For inasmuch as the divine entity is constituted here in terms of power, it is "blind," which is to say, it is devoid of awareness and thus of the capacity to intend or to freely decide. As such, it clearly cannot serve as an active agent vis-à-vis the human entity. But it can serve as a model, seeing that this role does not require the entity to possess the capability to intend or to freely decide. What is required is that the entity (in our case here it being the divine entity) should in its existence reflect a state of existence that overcomes what has been "diagnosed" as the fundamental predicament and this role is in no way undermined by the fact that the entity in question here is "blind." Thus, for example, if the perceived fundamental predicament within the dimension-of-power were, as we shall presently want to argue, a finitude of power, then the divine entity by possessing infinite power would serve as a model to the human entity. But not only is the divine entity excluded here from functioning as an active agent by the fact that it is "blind," the fact that it also constitutes itself in an ontological continuum with the human entity (and for that matter with the world at large) enables it to function as a model to the human entity. For to function as a model there must be a qualitative sameness between the entity that is to function as the model and the entity for which it functions as a model, the difference between the two being confined to a mere quantitative difference. Thus, we have here both a negative conclusion regarding the capability of the divine entity to function as an active agent and a positive conclusion as regards its capability to function as a model.

At the same time, however, we would also submit that within the dimension-of-consciousness the divine entity is likely to function primarily not as a model but as an active agent in bringing about the salvific/redemptive state, i.e., the state in which the perceived fundamental predicament is overcome. For, inasmuch as a divine entity constituted in terms of consciousness possesses awareness and consequently the capacity to freely intend and decide in relating towards the other (specifically, in our context here, the other being the human entity), it can function as an active agent in the bringing about of the salvific/redemptive state. At the same time, inasmuch as its ontological constitution implicates a "gap," an over-againstness, between it and the human entity (thus undermining any ontological continuum between itself and the human entity) and as such differentiating itself from the ontological constitution of the human entity in a qualitative and not merely in a quantitative sense, the feasibility of its functioning as a model to the human entity is, strictly speaking, cancelled out (indeed, as we shall see below when examining the expression of the religious phenomenon in Judaism, the call for *imitatio dei* does indeed raise a number of serious problems).

II

Paganism and the Hebrew Bible

Thus, to begin with, a good case can be made that all the various concrete, historical expressions of the religious phenomenon which are usually referred to in the Western World as pagan (an appellation that we will adopt here but without any trace of the negative evaluation that has been attached to it in the Western World because of the biblical orientation), as, for example, all aboriginal religions, African tribal religions, American-Indian religions, Ancient Near-Eastern religions, Hellenistic religions, and Asian religions, are expressions that formulate themselves exclusively in the context of the dimension-of-power, which is to say (as per our observation above that the kind of divine entity present in the formulation reflects the type of religion implicated) that they are expressions in whose formulation the divine entity constitutes itself in terms of power, i.e., as an It-god.[1]

Thus, the type of religion that constitutes itself in the context of the dimension-of-power can be readily encountered in the various concrete, historical religions that belong to pagan religion. And indeed, the expression of pagan religion can be encountered in the history of religion not only in its early stages but also throughout its progression up to and including our time, the era of modernity. Moreover, its expression is not confined to a peripheral, out-of-the-way corner of the world but is available globally, i.e., in all places on this earth. And this is so, not only because many of the concrete, historical expressions of pagan religion continue to be present, and indeed to prosper, today in many parts of the world but even in places where the secularism characterizing modernity has taken hold as, for example, in the Western World, this in no way cancels out the orientation, the *Weltanschauung*, of pagan religion but on the contrary expresses it to the fullest extent. For a good case can be made that the *Weltanschauung* of the secularism of modernity is, in its very essence, one and the same as the

Weltanschauung of pagan religion. True, the *Weltanschauung* of the secularism of modernity is no doubt much more sophisticated, substantial, and dependable than the various concrete, historical expressions of pagan religion (particularly when taken on the level of the common man and in a literal sense) but in its essence it is the same as the *Weltanschauung* of pagan religion, seeing that both formulate themselves in terms of the dimension-of-power—in both reality, in the last analysis, is perceived as constituting itself in terms of power and in which, therefore, all relations are relations of utilization, i.e., transactions of power.

Thus, if we are right to claim that pagan religions ground themselves in the dimension-of-power,[2] then there can be no question that we are provided with ample opportunities to encounter the type of religion that grounds itself in the dimension-of-power throughout the history of religion from its inception (which may well have coincided with the emergence of the human entity in the evolutionary process) to the present day.

Similarly, a good case can be made that the other alternative type of religion, the type of religion that grounds itself in the dimension-of-consciousness, can also be encountered in concrete historical religions and as such that it too is not merely a speculative hypothetical possibility but a type that finds concrete expression within the history of religion. Thus, we would submit that there are four concrete historical expressions of the religious phenomenon in which this type of religion can be encountered. Putting the matter more precisely, we would amend the foregoing to say that there is an originary concrete historical expression, that being the prophetic strand within the Hebrew bible, and in consequence of this three additional offshoot concrete historical religions, namely, that of Halachic Judaism, Christianity and Islam—the three "daughter religions" emanating from the religion of the Hebrew Bible.[3]

It should be noted, however, that in contradistinction to the type of religion that grounds itself in the dimension-of-power, i.e., pagan religion, the type of religion that grounds itself in the dimension-of-consciousness, i.e., biblical religion, appears relatively late in the history of religion (it certainly does not appear at the inception of that history—in the history of religion it is a "Johnny come lately") and when it does appear in the history of religion, it manifests itself in a relatively very small number of concrete historical religions (though it is true that through the successful missionizing activity of Christianity and even more so of Islam it does eventually become to a large extent globalized). But while this in no way undermines the claim that this type is not a mere speculative hypothesis but a type that can be encountered in concrete historical religions (seeing that the validation of this claim requires only that it be possible to encounter this type in a single concrete historical religion), the fact that it appears late necessarily implicates that this type of religion, i.e., biblical religion, inevitably comes into being within a context in which the presence of the type of religion that grounds itself in the dimension-of-power, i.e., pagan religion, is already there. It cannot express itself in a context that is neutral, that is, so to speak, virgin soil as far as the expression of religion is concerned.

But if this be the case, then it follows that theoretically there are two options by which the type that grounds itself in the dimension-of-consciousness can proceed. It can either totally abrogate the dimension-of-power, replacing it with the exclusive presence of the dimension-of-consciousness, or it may add itself to the dimension-of-power, thus presenting us with a cohabitation of the two dimensions. Now, we would submit that it is the second and not the first alternative that one encounters in the Hebrew Bible and in the three concrete historical religions emanating from it—in all these instances one can encounter both the type that grounds itself in the dimension-of-power and the type that grounds itself in the dimension-of-consciousness. But clearly, such a claim requires substantiation (and, indeed, an assessment of the feasibility of such a cohabitation) and so it is to this task that we must now turn.

The first source that we are going to focus on is the Hebrew Bible. This is so not only because it is the originary source where such a cohabitation can be encountered but also, and indeed much more significantly, because, as we shall presently see, it is the place (precisely in being the originary source) where the basic strategy underlying the attempt to overcome the problematics implicated in bringing about such a cohabitation is worked out. (The three subsequent religious formulations, i.e., those constituting Halachic Judaism, Christianity, and Islam, adopt in the main the essential thrust of this strategy though they then proceed to fashion it so that it can cope with the particular circumstances that confront each one of them—adopting to exile-existence in the case of Halachic Judaism and to the vocation of missionizing to a pagan world in the case of Christianity and Islam).

Thus, we would submit that the presence of the two types of religion, i.e., the religion that grounds itself in the dimension-of-consciousness and the religion that grounds itself in the dimension-of-power, is reflected in the two major strands identified by biblical scholarship and referred to as the prophetic and priestly strands—the type that grounds itself in the dimension-of-consciousness being reflected in the prophetic strand and the type that grounds itself in the dimension-of-power being reflected in the priestly strand. For we would contend that the various aspects, i.e., assertions, descriptions, claims, that are encountered respectively in the prophetic strand and the priestly strand point respectively to the type of religion that grounds itself in the dimension-of-consciousness and to the type of religion that grounds itself in the dimension-of-power inasmuch as they can receive a rationale and a justification only in the context of the dimension-of-consciousness and the dimension-of-power respectively. And that this is so should be fairly clear, we believe, once these aspects are presented.[4]

Thus, that the prophetic strand reflects the type of religion that grounds itself in the dimension-of-consciousness can, for example, be seen in that in the prophetic strand, 1) the authentic relating of the human entity towards the divine entity, i.e., the authentic mode of worship, is in the nature of a response to a demand emanating from the divine entity rather than in being initiated by the human entity towards a passive divine entity in order to utilize through its manipulation the greater power of the divine entity to its own advantage. 2) The content of the demand issuing from the diving entity is for the human entity to pursue justice towards its fellow-human entity. Put more precisely, the content of the demand issuing from the divine entity is in its essence a demand to be affirmed, a demand that is dictated by the divine entity being ontologically constituted as a pure Thou entity. But this, in turn, when applied to the fellow-human entity is refracted into a demand to act justly towards him/her, seeing that the fellow-human entity is ontologically constituted as an It/Thou entity and as such by virtue of its being constituted as a Thou, he/she demands affirmation while at the same time, by virtue of being constituted as an It, he/she also allows utilization thus resulting in utilization being allowed, but only when it remains within the bounds of fairness, i.e., of proportionality, which is tantamount to demanding that one should always act justly towards one's fellow-human entity. 3) Although the vertical relating to the divine entity is essentially mediated through the horizontal relating to the fellow-human entity, a direct, vertical relating to the divine entity is possible on occasion, but such relating is conveyed only through speech, i.e., by words, and not through action, i.e., by physical manipulations (physical manipulations being constituted by power while words in their essence, i.e., words as bearers of meaning rather than as formations in sound, are constituted by consciousness). 4) The divine entity communicates and discloses itself to the human, doing this, however, solely by speech. Thus, the phenomenon of revelation is not only possible but actualized—indeed, there is much more of the divine entity being in search of the human entity in the prophetic strand of the Hebrew Bible than of the human entity being in search of the divine entity. 5) On the occasions when the divine entity manifests itself in action rather than in speech, it manifests itself in history rather than in nature and consequently sanctifications are not of space but of time (thus, for example, the sanctification of what came to be known as the pilgrimage holidays, i.e., the holidays of Pessach, Shavuot, and Succot, is not by virtue of their linkage to the agricultural cultivation of the land but by virtue of their association with certain historical events). 6) As expressed so powerfully in the prophet's rejection of the sacrificial and fasting rituals (see Isaiah II 58:1-8), the efficacy of the rituals, i.e., of the relating to the divine, can be effected only when they are accompanied with having the right intention and with relating justly to one's fellow humans and not by the mechanical precision of performing the prescribed acts of the ritual. 7) Lastly, the divine entity is given a personal name, i.e., Yahweh.

Likewise, that the priestly strand reflects the type of religion that grounds itself in the dimension-of-power can, for example, be seen in that in the priestly strand, 1) the relating to the divine entity, i.e., the mode of worship, is exclusively in terms of action and not of speech as can be seen in the main, perhaps the only, form of relating that is obtainable here, i.e., the sacrificial cult (indeed, as pointed out by Yehezkel Kaufmann, the sacrificial ritual was performed in the Temple in complete silence with no accompaniment of verbal prayers or blessings). 2) The divine entity here is, on the whole, on the receiving end being rather passive. The initiative and the action come from the side of the human entity. We certainly do not encounter here the ongoing communication initiated from the divine entity to the human entity that we encounter in the prophetic strand. We do not encounter here the phenomenon of revelation in the authentic sense. Indeed, when the human entity requires information from the divine entity the mechanism by which it is effected is not through the transmission of the word in a personal encounter but rather through the utilization by the human (i.e., by the High Priest) of the Urim VeTumim—a mechanical means initiated and operated by the human entity by which the information from the divine entity is obtained. 3) The efficacy of relating to the divine here lies not in the human entity possessing the right intentions but rather in the accuracy and precision by which the acts through which the human entity is to relate to the divine entity (e.g., the act of animal sacrifice) are carried out. 4) The bifurcation of the domain of reality into pure and impure or sacred and profane realms. 5) The sanctification of specific localities in space (e.g., the land of Israel, the Temple in Jerusalem) rather than of specific events in time (e.g., exodus from Egypt, the revelation at Sinai) resulting from encountering the divine in nature rather than in history. 6) The divine entity is given merely a generic name, i.e., Eloha or Elohim, signifying "the divine".

But if this be the case, then the question must inescapably arise as to how the Hebrew bible can possibly encompass both the prophetic and the priestly strands, seeing that the two dimensions, namely, the dimension-of-consciousness and the dimension-of-power, in which they respectively ground themselves are in so many respects contradictory? How can a head-on collision between the two strands be avoided? Our answer is that the Hebrew bible can hold together these two contradictory strands, avoiding a manifest collision between them (though by no means avoiding strong tensions between them) by, so to speak, refracting, i.e., bending or mitigating, the formulation of each strand towards the formulation of the other strand. Thus, the priestly strand refracts itself towards the prophetic strand by essentially adopting the stance of henotheism or of monolatery.[5] For as such, the priestly strand adopts a single divine entity and, perhaps even more significantly, a divine entity that appears to be a personal deity, an adoption which clearly signifies its deflection towards the prophetic strand, seeing that these two aspects constitute essential characteristics of the prophetic strand, i.e., the rejection of polytheism and the ensuing single deity being a personal entity. At the same time, the prophetic strand refracts itself towards the priestly strand by retaining the arrogation of power to the divine entity, now constituted as a personal entity (indeed the arrogation of power here is the arrogation of infinite power, of omnipotence, seeing that the divine signifies here ultimacy). Thus, taken at face value, these refractions as regards both the priestly and the prophetic strands do indeed seem to effect a convergence between the two strands. They certainly seem to neutralize the points where otherwise a head-on collision between the two strands would have been inevitably precipitated; indeed, we can make the point even more emphatically and say that they seem to deflect each strand towards embracing the essential attributes belonging to the other, the priestly strand embracing the oneness of the divine entity and its being a personal entity and the prophetic strand embracing the attribution of infinite power to the divine entity.

A more careful examination, however, of the aforementioned strategies used both in the priestly and in the prophetic strands would have led us to conclude that the convergence proffered by them is not really, in the last analysis, tenable. What the strategies here succeed in giving us is a good cosmetic job in papering over the contradictions between the two strands (and thus allowing the biblical redactor to hold on to both strands). But they do not succeed in giving us a convergence of the two strands that would substantively overcome their contradictions.

This is so in view of the following considerations. First, as regards the deflection of the priestly strand towards the prophetic strand as reflected in the henotheistic formulation, the oneness attributed to the divine entity here signifies merely the arithmetical notion of oneness but not its metaphysical notion, i.e., the notion of ultimacy. But as such the priestly strand remains with a divine entity that is merely penultimate and not ultimate as is the case with regard to the divine entity in the prophetic strand and consequently establishing any comparison between the two strands, leave alone establishing a sameness, as regards their respective divine entities, is not really valid. For notwithstanding the fact that now both strands are the same in acknowledging a single divine entity, they do not share sameness as regards what really counts with respect to the notion of the divine entity and that is whether or not it is accorded the same metaphysical status of ultimacy. Thus, even if the divine entity would have been ontologically constituted as a personal entity, as a Thou entity, in both the priestly and the prophetic strands, it would not have been the same divine entity, seeing that in the prophetic strand the divine entity as a personal entity is ultimate while in the priestly strand the divine entity as a personal entity is penultimate.

But moreover, one can argue that as penultimate the divine entity in the priestly strand cannot really be, in the last analysis, an authentic personal entity, an authentic Thou entity. For as penultimate the divine entity here is evidently quantified (it is less than the entity that is ultimate) and quantification is feasible only in the context of the dimension-of-power and not in the context of the dimension-of-consciousness. Thus, as a penultimate entity the divine entity here in the priestly strand remains within the dimension-of-power. Indeed, a more careful examination would show that in the priestly strand the divine entity is not really an authentic personal entity but merely a personified entity, namely, an entity that in its essence constitutes itself in terms of the dimension-of-power but to which we attribute certain characteristics belonging to a personal entity, such characteristics as, for example, possessing volition, feeling and thinking (such a process of personification being conveyed most succinctly by attributing a personal name to the entity). The divine entity is given the appearance of being constituted in terms of the dimension-of-consciousness while in truth it continues to constitute itself in terms of the dimension-of-power. That this is so can be seen in the all-important fact that beneath the veneer of the personal characteristics attributed to the divine entity, all the relations in which the divine entity here is implicated (to wit, all its relations to the human entity and, vice versa, all of the relations of the human entity to it) are, in the last analysis, relations of utilization, relations that arise exclusively in the context of the dimension-of-power. For inasmuch as nothing reveals more clearly the ontological constitution of an entity than the kind of relations in which it is implicated (one knows an entity most truthfully by its relations), the fact that the relations here belong to the dimension-of-power determines in the most incontrovertible manner that the divine entity here too constitutes itself ontologically in terms of the dimension-of-power. Thus, not only is the divine entity in the priestly strand not the same as the divine entity encountered in the prophetic strand because it is a penultimate entity while the divine entity in the prophetic strand is an ultimate entity, but because, in the last analysis, it constitutes itself in terms of the dimension-of-power, as an It-god (the divine entity being here penultimate, we do not capitalize the word "god") while the divine entity in the prophetic strand constitutes itself in terms of the dimension-of-consciousness, as a Thou-God (the divine entity being here ultimate, we do capitalize the word "god"). Clearly the strategy of resorting to henotheism or monolatery fails, in the last analysis, to establish a viable *modus vivendi* between the dimension-of-consciousness and the dimension-of-power, thus enabling a religious formulation to really hold on to both dimensions simultaneously without contradiction.

Indeed, already in classical biblical prophecy (namely, from the prophet Amos on) and subsequently also in the three "daughter religions" emanating from the Hebrew Bible, namely, Halachic Judaism, Christianity, and Islam, the resort to a henotheistic or monolateralist formulation is abandoned. Instead, what we encounter here is an authentic, full-fledged monotheistic formulation, seeing that, in contradistinction to the henotheistic or monolateralist formulation, the formulation here maintains that a particular divine entity (named in the Hebrew Bible by the personal name of Yahweh, thus indicating that it is a personal entity, a Thou-being) is the ultimate entity and in consequence the only divine entity. Yahweh is no longer the only divine entity merely for a particular nation, i.e., the people of Israel, thus recognizing the existence and legitimacy of other divine entities as regards other nations; Yahweh now is the only authentic divine entity existing, thus the only divine entity also as regards all other nations. Polytheism, the acknowledgement of a plurality of divine entities, is rejected and monotheism, the acknowledgement of a single divine entity for the whole of creation, is adopted.[6]

Now this means of course that in giving up the henotheistic and monolateralist formulations classical biblical prophecy and the three "daughter religions" can mitigate the potential conflict between the dimension-of-power and the dimension-of-consciousness (namely the potential conflict between elements of the pagan religion retained in their respective formulations and the revolutionary new perspective introduced by the prophetic strand) only from the side of the dimension-of-consciousness and not also from the side of the dimension-of-power, namely, only by "refracting" the dimension-of-consciousness towards the dimension-of-power but not in the reverse. This indeed is what takes place in all the above mentioned expressions of biblical religion—the divine entity taken as the ultimate entity within the context of the dimension-of-consciousness, thus the divine entity being constituted by its very essence as a person (this being the revolutionary innovative element introduced by the prophetic strand in the Hebrew Bible) is arrogated nonetheless power and being an ultimate entity it is indeed arrogated infinite power, omnipotence.[7]

Indeed, this arrogation of infinite power to the divine entity is very deeply ingrained (one is tempted to say inextricably ingrained) within the religious formulation of all the expressions of biblical religion. It seems to be an aspect that none of these formulations seems capable of abdicating regardless of how serious the problematic which the retention of this aspect may precipitate.[8]

In a way we can appreciate this insistence by the various religious traditions formulating themselves in the context of biblical religion on arrogating power to the divine entity, for from the vantage point of the religious enterprise the existence of the divine entity can have meaning and significance only if and to the extent that it has a role to play with respect to the human situation. A divine entity that has no contact, involvement, with the human can have no value or interest for the religious enterprise (see, for example, the failure of deism to prove itself viable within the domain of religion). For the religious enterprise is, so to speak, in the business of offering redemption/salvation to the human, which is to say, it is in the business of delineating for the human a form of existence in which what is perceived as the fundamental predicament in our present existence is overcome, and in this context the divine entity has per force a central role to play, thus impinging on the most fundamental level on the existence and destiny of the human (by and large the divine entity is an active agent in the economy of salvation/redemption though the extent and the nature of the activity implicated may well vary in the different religious formulations—minimally it may merely act as the model of the entity that exists in the state of salvation/redemption while maximally its activity is the sole factor by which the state of salvation/redemption is brought about). A detached, purely theoretical interest, pursued for its own sake, in establishing the existence of a divine entity and/or delineating its ontological constitution, i.e., describing its various attributes, may legitimately belong to the philosophic enterprise but not to the religious enterprise.

The question, however, whether the divine entity can in terms of its ontological constitution readily lend itself to being actively implicated in the overcoming of the human predicament, thus assuming a meaningful role within the religious enterprise, remains, of course, still to be determined and it is to this task that we must now turn.

The first thing to note in this connection is that for the divine entity to be actively implicated in the overcoming of what is perceived as the fundamental human predicament it has to satisfy two conditions—first, it must be capable of being aware of, indeed concerned with, the human situation and the fundamental predicament it implies, and secondly, it must possess the capacity to effectively impinge upon the enterprise of overcoming this predicament. Now this means that with respect to a divine entity (indeed, any entity) that constitutes itself exclusively in terms of consciousness, i.e., as a pure Thou, the first condition is readily satisfied, for after all, as a bearer of consciousness such a divine entity is clearly capable of being aware of and concerned with the human predicament. At the same time, however, the satisfaction of the second condition would seem to be, at least on first consideration, unfeasible, for by and large we would not be inclined to accept (again, at least on first consideration) that an entity constituted exclusively in terms of awareness, which is to say, an entity devoid of all power, could nonetheless be implicated as an effective agent in overcoming the state of affairs which is perceived to constitute the human predicament. In contradistinction to this, with respect to a divine entity that constitutes itself exclusively in terms of power, i.e., as a pure It, the reverse situation obtains, namely, the second condition can be readily satisfied, seeing that the divine entity here has power at its disposal while the first condition cannot be satisfied, seeing that power is blind moving inexorably and unaware of anything in its predetermined path. And of course, this in turn means that in the context of biblical religion the first condition but not, it would seem, the second condition can be satisfied, seeing that the distinctive mark characterizing biblical religion lies in the fact that the ultimate entity encountered in its context is a personal entity, while in the context of pagan religion the second condition but not the first condition can be satisfied, seeing that in the context of pagan religion the ultimate that is encountered is blind power, what the Greeks called *moira* and the Romans called *fatum* (by the way the Aristotelian god, though professedly constituted as self-contained in order to safeguard its perfection, is on a more fundamental level reflecting the essential feature characterizing the ultimate entity that is constituted in the context of paganism, i.e., the essential feature of blind power, which is its lack of awareness of, and thus concern with, the world, except that it reflects it in its static rather than in its dynamic state).[9]

Now, in view of this conclusion it should not be all that surprising to encounter in the various concrete, historical expressions of each of these two fundamental types of religious formulations, to wit, the pagan and the biblical religious formulations, a clear tendency to incorporate into their respective concrete, historical expressions the alternative missing factor—the pagan concrete, historical expressions incorporating the factor of personhood and the biblical concrete, historical expressions incorporating the factor of power—thus enabling them to satisfy both conditions and as such make their expressions religiously viable. Thus, it should not be surprising to see that the concrete, historical expressions as pagan religion personify the various manifestations of power in nature in their various pantheonic divine entities and that the concrete, historical expressions of biblical religion arrogate power to their personal divine entity. But is this move by both the concrete, historical expressions of pagan religion and those of biblical religion to incorporate the alternative additional factor into their respective formulations tenable? Well, there would seem to be some serious problems arising in connection with this move with respect to both the concrete, historical expressions of pagan religion and with respect to the concrete historical expressions of biblical religion.

Thus, with respect to the concrete, historical expressions of pagan religion, it should first be pointed out that the factor of personhood is introduced here not in connection with the entity that is ultimate but in connection with entities that are merely penultimate. Namely, it is only the penultimate expressions of power, to wit, power as it manifests itself in the various forces of nature, that are personified here; power in its ultimate expression, the *moira* of the Greeks and the *fatum* of the Romans, is in no way personified here. And, this being the case, one may well be tempted to argue that the failure to establish the presence of personhood with respect to the entity that is ultimate, establishing it only with respect to penultimate entities, is tantamount, in the last analysis, to undermining, for all intents and purposes, any bearing that the introduction of the factor personhood may have here on the issue of ensuring the religious viability of the various concrete, historical expressions of pagan religion. For what our foregoing deliberation seemed to imply was that in order to establish the religious viability of any formulation the implication of both the factor of power and the factor of personhood is required and that, indeed, their implication has to be specifically with respect to the entity that is ultimate and not just penultimate.

True, it is possible to respond to this point by arguing that the requirement implied in our foregoing deliberation that the arrogation of both factors is to be to an entity that is ultimate and not merely penultimate was introduced because of the clear assumption present in out deliberation that we are to deal here with the overcoming of a predicament that is ultimate and not merely penultimate (seeing that by our very delineation of the enterprise of religion, religion is to be implicated in the overcoming of predicaments that are ultimate and not merely penultimate) and that clearly such an overcoming would implicate an agent, to wit, a divine entity, that must itself be an ultimate and not merely a penultimate entity. But evidently, this assumption cannot be taken at face value when applied to pagan religion—the situation here is more complex. Thus, on the one hand, pagan religion does indeed recognize an entity that is ultimate which as such is, in the full significance of the notion, its authentic divine entity, this entity being that of blind power as such. But, on the other hand, this ultimate entity (for example this *moira* or *fatum*) is not given in pagan religion the role of being the active agent in overcoming that which is perceived in its context as the ultimate in the sense of being the fundamental predicament afflicting the human—its role remains that of the passive, albeit ultimate, source which can provide, when properly manipulated, that which is needed to overcome the predicament. The role of the active agent in overcoming the fundamental predicament is assigned in pagan religion to penultimate entities, the penultimate expressions of power as manifested in the various forces of nature. Pagan religion can do this because inasmuch as it formulates itself in terms of the dimension-of-power, it is to be expected that both what it identifies as the fundamental predicament of the human entity and commensurate to this what it can offer to the human entity by way of overcoming this predicament (i.e., the redemption/salvation that it can offer) will be constituted in terms of power. Now, power is by its very essence quantifiable and this, in turn, means that both the predicament and commensurately to it the overcoming of the predicament can be formulated here in terms of degree, namely the predicament signifying a low level of power while its overcoming signifying an increase in the level of power.[10]

Now, in such a context the agent implicated in bringing about the overcoming of the predicament can indeed be a penultimate entity as long as it possesses more power than the entity bearing the predicament and, this being the case, any one of the various forces of nature could be implicated as the agent here and consequently attributing personhood to any one of these forces, as is done in the case of the pantheonic gods, would satisfy after all the demand that the agent implicated in the overcoming of the predicament must be an entity that possesses both power and personhood. Thus, with respect to any religious phenomenon that formulates itself in the context of the dimension-of-power, as is the case with respect to any formulation of pagan religion, the attribution of personhood to penultimate entities rather than to the ultimate entity would not undermine the religious viability of the formulation.

The viability of the formulation of pagan religion, however, may still be undermined by yet another, and indeed a more fundamental, objection that can be raised against it. Namely, it can be legitimately objected that the attribution of personhood to the various forces of nature in the pantheonic gods, is, in the last analysis, not really an authentic personhood but merely a personification. This is so because while the pantheonic gods are presented here as being aware of humans and indeed as possessing the various attributes of consciousness encountered in the human such as emotions (e.g., anger, jealousy, vengeance), desires (e.g., lusting, coveting) and thinking (e.g., scheming, calculating), in essence they remain entities that can relate to others and that can be related to by others only in terms of utilization. They remain entities devoid of the capability to extend affirmation and as such they are in essence It entities i.e., entities constituted exclusively in terms of power, even though humans by virtue of their imagination can relate to them *as if* they were also Thou entities, i.e., entities endowed with personhood (an analogous situation can be encountered in the way children may relate to their teddy bears or in the way some grownups may relate to their favorite car or sailboat, the personification here manifesting itself in, among other ways, the bestowal of proper names on these impersonal entities). Thus, the attribution of personhood here is, in the last analysis, merely cosmetic—it may possess a psychological by not an ontological significance.

Now, this conclusion would be a most serious challenge to the religious viability of the formulation of pagan religion if this formulation really required that the agent implicated in the overcoming of the fundamental predicament it addresses (the agent here being a penultimate divine entity) be authentically a person and not merely a personification of power. For clearly, authentic personhood is not delivered within the formulation of pagan religion. However, a good case can be made that the formulation of pagan religion does not really require that its penultimate divine agent, the agent implicated in the overcoming of the fundamental predicament which it addresses, be endowed with authentic personhood and consequently the failure to attribute authentic personhood to the divine entities in the formulation of pagan religion should not undermine the viability of the formulation after all. For, inasmuch as the class of pagan religions, by their very essence, formulate themselves in the context of the dimension-of-power, they deal exclusively (both in their formulation of the fundamental predicament and in their formulation of its overcoming) in terms of transactions of power, which is to say, they deal exclusively in terms of relations of utilization and in such a context there is absolutely no need for the agent which would be implicated here (i.e., the penultimate divine entity) to be endowed in its ontological structure with authentic personhood. The need to have the penultimate divine agent as a person, i.e., as an entity possessing awareness of others, is purely psychological and a psychological need (in clear contradistinction to an ontological need) can indeed be satisfied by attributing the mere appearance of personhood, i.e., by attributing mere personification. Thus, since in the context of pagan religion there is no need for attributing personhood to the ontological structure of the agent implicated in the overcoming of the fundamental predicament (i.e., to the ontological structure of a penultimate divine entity), the merely cosmetic attribution of personhood, i.e., the mere attribution of personification to the pantheonic gods, should not undermine the viability of the formulation of pagan religion. At the same time, however, to the extent that there is a psychological need, the attribution of what is a mere personification should be quite adequate to satisfy this need.[11]

Turning now to assessing the introduction of the factor of power into the formulation of biblical religion, the first thing to note is that the context associated with biblical religion is radically different from that associated with pagan religion. This is to be expected, seeing that pagan religion formulates itself in terms of the dimension-of-power while biblical religion formulates itself in terms of dimension-of-consciousness. Indeed, this fundamental bifurcation directly precipitates the all-important difference whereby while all entities constituting themselves in terms of the dimension-of-power are quantifiable (seeing that power, by its very essence, lends itself to being more and less) and therefore lend themselves to being graded in terms of the degree of power they possess, all entities constituting themselves in terms of the dimension-of-consciousness are not quantifiable (seeing that consciousness, by its very essence, is all or none) and therefore do not lend themselves to being graded in terms of the consciousness they possess—one is either conscious or not conscious; there are no degrees of consciousness.[12] And this, in turn, means that we cannot really have in the context of the dimension-of-consciousness a penultimate entity, seeing that with respect to consciousness there is no more and less. Indeed, within the context of the dimension-of-consciousness, ultimacy does not signify infinity but exclusivity. In this context, by saying that an entity is ultimate we mean to say that it constitutes itself exclusively in terms of consciousness without the admixture of any other "stuff" as, for example, power—namely, that it constitutes itself as a pure Thou. And this being the case, arrogating power to a divine entity (i.e., to a god), when "divinity" signifies here ultimacy in the context of the dimension-of-consciousness (i.e., god with a capital g), is a contradiction in terms. Clearly, the situation here is radically different from the situation we encounter in the context of the dimension-of-power. There it was feasible, in principle, to allow participation in another dimension to the entity that was taken as ultimate in that context; here it is not (and, by the way, neither is it possible to have in the context of the dimension-of-consciousness anything similar with respect to the factor of power that could parallel the refraction of personhood into personification done with respect to the factor of consciousness in the context of the dimension-of-power—power unlike consciousness does not lend itself to being presented in an "as if" manner).

But not only does the arrogation of power to a divine entity which by its very essence constitutes itself as a Thou, i.e., in terms of consciousness, of personhood (as is the case in the formulations of the concrete historical expressions of biblical religion), undermines the ultimacy of such a divine entity, it also undermines two further very fundamental and indeed essential aspects associated with the formulations of biblical religion. These two aspects are the wholly otherness characterizing the divine entity with respect to the world and its closely linked aspect of the theistic, in contradistinction to the pantheistic, relatedness of the divine entity to the world (theism signifying here the transcendence of the divine entity with respect to the totality of the world, i.e., its existence over-against the world, separated from it by an unbridgeable "gap," and pantheism in signifying the identity of the divine entity with the totality of the world).

Thus, as regards the first aspect, the arrogation of power to a divine entity taken as an ultimate personal entity, as a pure Thou, as it is done in all three of the concrete, historical expressions of biblical religion, necessarily implicates the undermining of this divine entity as an entity that ontologically constitutes itself exclusively in terms of consciousness (which is to say as the entity that is the ultimate entity within the context of the dimension-of-consciousness) and as such as an entity that is qualitatively different in its ontological constitution—and in this sense an entity that is wholly other—from the ontological constitution characterizing the sum total of all entities constituting the world, i.e., from the ontological constitution characterizing both inanimate and animate (including human) nature. The divine entity in being constituted here in terms of both consciousness and power, i.e., in being ontologically constituted as an It/Thou rather than as a pure Thou entity, is given an ontological constitution that is, qualitatively speaking, the same as the ontological constitution possessed by the human entity.[13] And while with respect to inanimate nature, it is true that a qualitative difference exists, seeing that the entities of inanimate nature do not ontologically constitute themselves in terms of the dimension-of-consciousness but only in terms of the dimension-of-power (i.e., that they ontologically constitute themselves as It entities), still a degree of sameness remains inasmuch as both the entities of inanimate nature and the divine entity here share a common denominator in that both ontologically constitute themselves in terms of the dimension-of-power, albeit that in the case of the entities of inanimate nature it is exclusively so while in the case of the divine entity here it is only partially so. As such, the arrogation of power to the divine entity, as it is done in all three of the concrete, historical expressions of biblical religion, must necessarily implicate the invalidity of also attributing to such a divine entity the aspect of wholly otherness.

And as regards the second aspect, the arrogation of power to the divine entity, i.e., to the entity that is an ultimate entity and therefore the arrogation not merely of power as such but of infinite power, similarly undermines the feasibility of the divine entity existing over-against the world, of there being an unbridgeable "gap" between the divine entity and the world. This is so because of two considerations. First, inasmuch as power by its very essence constitutes itself as a continuum, it abhors and cannot accept any discontinuity, any "gap" with respect to itself—"nature (the expression *par excellence* of power) abhors a vacuum." As such, any entity (and this would include the divine entity), to the extent that it constitutes itself in terms of power, would necessarily find itself, to that extent, in a continuum with all other manifestations of power, namely, with all other entities to the extent that they constitute themselves in terms of power. Thus, inasmuch as the divine entity in the concrete, historical expressions of biblical religion constitutes itself in part in terms of power, in terms of that part it must be in a continuum with all other entities that constitute themselves either exclusively (e.g., the entities of inanimate nature) or partially (e.g., the human entities) in terms of power, which is to say that in terms of the element of power that is present in its ontological constitution, such a divine entity must be in a pantheistic and not in a theistic relation to the world—the "gap" between the divine entity and the human entity and, indeed, between the divine entity and nature is cancelled out here. Secondly, if the divine entity were to relate to the world theistically rather than pantheistically, then it would seem that inescapably such a divine entity could not possibly possess power to an infinite degree but only to a finite degree. Indeed, maintaining that the divine entity possesses infinite power and that at the same time it is relating to the world theistically would confront us with an irreconcilable contradiction. For how can the divine entity possess infinite power and at the same time have the entities of inanimate nature, entities that also possess power, be separate and distinct from it? Surely, in such a situation the power possessed by the divine entity cannot possibly be infinite, seeing that there is additional power present, which it does not possess. Certainly, the main thrust of St. Anselm's ontological argument, though obviously somewhat modified in its terminology, should be applicable here. Namely, we can certainly readily conceive of another entity that would embrace both the divine entity and the entities of inanimate and animate nature and thus clearly coming to possess more power than the power possessed by the original divine entity, and as such this would clearly negate the validity of the claim that the power in the possession of the original divine entity is infinite and that as such that entity is truly divine, if the notion of the divine is to signify ultimacy.

Thus, the arrogation of power to the divine entity in the three concrete, historical expressions of biblical religion, i.e., in Judaism, Christianity, and Islam, must inevitably precipitate, in principle, an untenable state of affairs. True, religious communities can, in their concrete religious life, live with formulations that are, in the last analysis, logically inconsistent. Indeed it is this that allows all three concrete historical expressions of biblical religion to arrogate power to their respective divine entities even though these divine entities, taken as ultimate entities, are being constituted, by their very essence, in the context of the dimension-of-consciousness, which is to say, as personal entities, i.e., as Thou-entities. But when approaching those religious communities from the theological perspective, namely, when trying to grasp the structures and contents of their respective faiths from an intellectual/rational vantage point, as we are trying to do here, logical inconsistencies cannot be papered over and conveniently ignored. They have to be resolved.

Now it would seem to us that the only way by which these inconsistencies can be resolved is by negating the arrogation of power (no matter how minimal the arrogation is) to the divine entity. Within the context of the dimension-of-consciousness the divine entity must constitute itself as totally powerless. But would not this render the divine entity completely ineffectual and thus irrelevant to the religious enterprise? For what role can such a divine entity play in the drama of salvation/redemption? What function can such a divine entity carry out in this context, seeing that it is devoid of all power? Indeed, should we not concede that the concrete, historical expressions of biblical religion, in introducing into the religious enterprise a divine entity that constitutes itself in its very essence as a personal entity, i.e., as a Thou-entity, had no choice but to pay the price of inconsistency in preserving the arrogation of power to that divine entity if the relevancy to the religious enterprise of such a divine entity, i.e., a divine entity which by its very essence is a Thou-entity, was to be preserved?

Our response to this is that the consideration put forth here against divesting the divine entity of power does indeed apply to the relevancy of the divine entity when the impact of its functioning is to take place in the context of the dimension-of-power. For here indeed, the absence of power precludes the very possibility of functioning and consequently an entity devoid of power cannot possibly be relevant. Thus, indeed, a divine entity devoid of power is clearly irrelevant as far as the sphere of nature is concerned. Such a divine entity, for example, cannot be a creator nor can it be providential.[14] But when the function of the divine entity is relegated to the context of the dimension-of-consciousness, the Thou-dimension, divesting the divine entity of power should in no way undermine the feasibility of its function. For in this context the efficacy and, indeed, the feasibility of divine functioning is in no way dependent on the availability of power—in this context a divine entity devoid of all power can nonetheless function most effectively.

Indeed, we would submit that there are two very significant functions that a divine entity constituting itself exclusively in terms of the Thou-dimension, i.e., constituting itself as a pure Thou entity (and thus being completely devoid of power), could nonetheless render to the human entity. One of these functions delineates itself in the context of the ontological domain while the other delineates itself in the context of the ethical domain. Thus, with respect to the function that delineates itself in the context of the ontological domain, a persuasive case can be made that in order for the Thou-dimension (i.e., the dimension implicating consciousness or, more to the point as far as our case here is concerned, self-consciousness) to come into existence in an entity and, indeed, be sustained within its existence, an extension of affirmation to it from the outside is a condition *sine qua non*. And, needless to say, the source for such affirmation, i.e., the entity that could provide the required affirmation, must of course itself be already ontologically constituted, wholly or only in part, in terms of the Thou-dimension. Now, clearly, a divine entity that constitutes itself exclusively in terms of the Thou-dimension can be the source that could extend the required affirmation. The dimension-of-power can play no role here and so the fact that the divine entity is devoid of all power would in no way undermine its capacity to play a role with respect to the human entity. Indeed, it cannot preclude its capacity to address and satisfy the most fundamental and essential need in the human entity, inasmuch as it constitutes itself as a Thou, namely, the need to be affirmed which provides the feasibility for the human entity as a Thou to come into existence and maintain itself within it.

And with respect to the second function, the function that delineates itself in the ethical domain, an equally persuasive case can be made that if (as we have tried to argue for in a different place) the ethical enterprise is to be seen as the enterprise which undertakes to evaluate/judge the acts of entities from the vantage point of the notion of justice, in other words, where the criterion by which the evaluation/judgment formulates itself is provided by the notion of justice (justice being taken here to signify the safeguarding or the attaining of a proper, i.e., fair, balance between the It and the Thou dimensions, the two dimensions in terms of which the ontological constitution of all entities subject to the evaluation/judgment of such an ethical enterprise must be constituted), a divine entity constituted as a pure Thou entity can indeed be seen to play a significant and all-important role, and this notwithstanding the fact that the divine entity here would be totally devoid of power.[15] Now, within the context of such an ethical enterprise, the divine entity constituting itself. For its role here would be that of, so to speak, leveling the playing fields between the dimension-of-power and the dimension-of-consciousness with regard to their respective capacities to determine the acts of the human entity, thus safeguarding that the ethical evaluation of these acts will be fair and just. This role is necessary, we would want to argue, because the "stuff" in terms of which the It-dimension and the Thou-dimension constitute themselves, to wit, power and consciousness respectively, possess markedly different characteristics which in consequence precipitate a significant imbalance between the two dimensions with regard to their respective capabilities to assert themselves and guide the acting of the human entity. Thus, power does not in any way implicate, leave alone depend upon, any outside source for its coming into existence or for sustaining itself within it; it is completely self-contained—a being-in-itself. Indeed, if anything, it is "imperialistic", i.e., ever striving to incorporate into itself more and more power (power being in its very essence quantifiable, such imperialistic aggrandizement is readily feasible with respect to it), thus expressing itself not only as a being-in-itself but also (and this is much more to the point we are trying to make here) as a being-for-itself. In contradistinction to this, consciousness by its very essence is dependent for its coming into existence and sustaining itself in it upon an external source that can extend to it affirmation (and as already noted, the external source here which is to extend the affirmation must clearly be an entity which itself is being constituted, at least in part, in terms of consciousness, i.e., as a Thou). As such, to the extent that an entity constitutes itself in terms of consciousness rather than of power (i.e., that it constitutes itself as a Thou rather than as an It), it would express itself as a being-for-another.[16] And given this disparity in the attributes characterizing power and consciousness respectively (the former being self-oriented, self-sufficient, aggressive and the latter being other-oriented, other-dependent, passive), a leveling of the playing field, so to speak, is clearly required if the attainment of justice, i.e., the establishment of a fair balance between the dimension-of-power and the dimension-of-consciousness, is to have a chance of being realized by the human entity.

But such a leveling, in turn, clearly implicates that two stipulations will have been met. First is the stipulation already raised when discussing the role of the divine entity vis-à-vis the human entity in the ontological domain, namely, the stipulation requiring that affirmation be extended to the human entity. For without such extension of affirmation the human entity would not be able to incorporate and retain within its ontological constitution the dimension-of-consciousness in addition to its incorporating the dimension-of-power, and consequently it could not function as the agent that can attain justice which, in turn, would be tantamount to abrogating the very applicability of the notion of justice, seeing that it is only the human entity (being the only entity that ontologically constitutes itself in terms of both the dimension-of-power and the dimension-of-consciousness, i.e. as an It/Thou entity) that can provide, so to speak, the arena in which the notion of justice can arise. Clearly, meeting this stipulation is a necessary condition if a leveling of the playing field is to take place. But, at the same time, it is not a sufficient condition. An additional, second stipulation must be met. For inasmuch as the dimension-of-power is "imperialistic", i.e., self-assertive and proactive, while the dimension-of-consciousness is other-oriented and passive, it means that even though both dimensions may be incorporated within the ontological constitution of the human entity, if they are left to themselves (i.e., if no assistance from the outside is available), the dimension-of-power will dominate and suppress the dimension-of-consciousness, resulting in its being the dimension which dictates and determines the kind of activity to be pursued by the human entity. To preclude this pitfall, an entity placed overagainst the human entity and constituting itself (at least in part) as a Thou is called for, seeing that such an entity could not only extend affirmation to the human entity but could also remind it that it is constituted not only in terms of the dimension-of-power but also in terms of the dimension-of-consciousness, thus challenging the human entity to give the dimension-of-consciousness its due input in determining its actions and thus safeguarding for the human entity the possibility of truly acting in accordance with the criterion of justice, which is to say, acting in accordance with a fair balance between the two dimensions when both have equal input in determining its actions. Now, certainly the divine entity constituting itself as a pure Thou could be that outside source that could meet and satisfy these two stipulations. And this being the case, one could clearly conclude that a divine entity, even though it be totally devoid of possessing power, could nonetheless play an essential role vis-à-vis the human entity both in the ontological and in the ethical domains. Thus, we would be justified in claiming that a divine entity constituting itself as a pure Thou (i.e., constituting itself exclusively in terms of personhood) can nevertheless function meaningfully, indeed most meaningfully, in the context of the religious phenomenon.

Still one could raise a serious objection to our claim on the ground that the role of the divine entity vis-à-vis the human entity as delineated here is by no means a role that can be provided only by the divine entity. True, this role can be provided by an entity constituting itself exclusively in terms of the Thou-dimension (i.e., in terms of the dimension-of-consciousness), thus by a divine entity constituting itself as a pure Thou. But it can also be provided by an entity that constitutes itself only in part in terms of the Thou-dimension, which is to say that a fellow human entity constituting itself as an It/Thou entity could also provide this role. Namely, to provide this role the presence of the Thou-dimension in an outside source is indeed required, but it is not required that it be exclusively the only dimension presented. But if this be the case, then the significance of there being a divine entity constituting itself as a pure Thou is greatly diminished if not indeed abrogated altogether. For the need for a divine entity being constituted as a pure Thou becomes now dispensable and thus, in the last analysis, superfluous—the drama of the religious phenomenon can play itself out without implicating the presence of a divine entity constituted as a pure Thou.

It would seem to us, however, that on closer reflection one could overcome this objection and reaffirm the need for implicating specifically a divine entity constituted as a pure Thou rather than merely a fellow human entity. This is so because while the human entity can indeed take the place of a divine entity constituted as a pure Thou in extending affirmation to its fellow human entity and indeed in challenging it to give its Thou-dimension its due say in determining its conduct, such a replacement harbors within itself a very serious flaw which, in the last analysis, undermines its validity. The flaw lies in the fact that in contradistinction to the divine entity here which ontologically constitutes itself exclusively in terms of the Thou-dimension, the human entity ontologically constitutes itself only partially in terms of the Thou-dimension, namely, it lies in the fact that the ontological constitution of the human entity encompasses not only the Thou-dimension but also in addition the It-dimension. For as such, the viability of the human entity as a provider of the necessary affirmation is seriously compromised in two ways. First, it is compromised because in encompassing the It-dimension the human entity must necessarily exist within the flux and as such it can be, and in its case it indeed is, contingent, namely, an entity that inescapably must enter and exit existence and this, in turn, means that it must necessarily implicate the prior existence of a fellow human entity, seeing that only as such can it be provided with the affirmation necessary for it to come into existence. And this, in turn, would clearly precipitate the serious problematic of infinite regress (namely, how could any human entity come into existence to begin with?). Secondly, it is being compromised because, in being constituted as an It/Thou entity, the human entity is continuously given the option of expressing itself either in terms of its It-dimension or in terms of its Thou-dimension and this means that its extension of affirmation and challenge to its fellow human becomes iffy. Thus, there can be no assurance that it would be feasible to bring into existence a human entity, to the extent that it is to be ontologically constituted in terms of the Thou-dimension, nor that it can be sustained in existence nor indeed provided with the possibility to establish justice.[17] At the same time, in contradistinction to this, when the human entity is replaced as the source of the affirmation by a divine entity which is ontologically constituted as a pure Thou entity, this flaw in either of its two expressions is avoided. For in not being ontologically constituted in any way, shape or manner, in terms of the It-dimension, the divine entity here does not exist within the flux of time (it exists in a state of eternity in the sense of being a state that transcends, i.e., that lies beyond, outside, the flow of time) and in consequence of this is not an entity that actually does (or indeed has to) come into or exit from existence thus precluding the problematic of infinite regress, nor is it an entity that has the option not to extend its affirmation to an other thus precluding the problematic that at any given time there could be the possibility of affirmation not being available. Clearly, it is only when we have as the source of the required affirmation a divine entity constituted as a pure Thou entity and not a human entity constituted as an It/Thou entity that we can have a source that is reliable and will always be available thus a source that can satisfactorily account for the coming into existence of the human entity (insofar as it constitutes itself in terms of the Thou-dimension) and its being sustained on an ongoing basis within that existence.

Resorting to a divine entity being constituted as a pure Thou to provide the required affirmation for the human entity (insofar as it constitutes itself in terms of the Thou-dimension) to come into and be sustained within existence and indeed enable it to establish justice precipitates, however, what may appear to be an equally serious problematic of its own. For such a move would inevitably include the implication that the existence of the divine entity precedes the existence of the human entity. And since the human entity is the only other kind of entity that constitutes itself in terms of the Thou-dimension (the fact that it so constitutes itself only partially does in no way affect our concerns here), the divine entity in its existence prior to the coming into existence of the human entity must clearly be alone as a Thou entity, i.e., the only entity constituting itself in terms of the Thou-dimension. Now, this would clearly precipitate a serious problem from the vantage point of the Thou-dimension (though admittedly not from the vantage point of the It-dimension, seeing that a divine entity constituting itself as a pure Thou, which is to say, constituting itself as an entity which in no way incorporates in its ontological constitution any aspects of the It-dimension, does not and, indeed, cannot exist within the flux, and consequently the very issues of coming into existence or being sustained within it are inapplicable to it). For in the context of the Thou-dimension an entity comes into existence, i.e., arises as a Thou entity, and indeed sustains itself in that existence not singly but in twos. The primary and fundamental unit here is a twosome and not a single entity—in the context of the Thou-dimension, it takes two entities in tandem to come into existence and to sustain themselves within it (in this context it takes two to tango). And this of course implicates that a divine entity constituting itself as a Thou entity cannot come into existence or sustain itself within it singly. It requires the companionship of another Thou entity. Now, seeing that the only other Thou entity available is the human entity (as already noted, the fact that the human entity constitutes itself only partially as a Thou entity does not cancel its effectiveness as a Thou entity for our consideration here), does of course mean that a divine entity that is to constitute itself as a Thou entity can come into existence and sustain itself within it only in companionship with the coming into existence of the human entity (indeed, the phenomenon of religion and thus the very notion of a divine entity arise only with the coming into existence of the human entity—before the appearance of the human entity there was no religion to begin with).

But would this not seem to imply that the divine entity here is a dependent and finite entity inasmuch as its existence depends on the commensurate existence of a human entity, an entity that is clearly a finite entity (after all the human entity has not been in existence from the very beginning of time; indeed, if anything, it comes into existence very late in the span of evolutionary time)? Thus, inasmuch as the divine entity's coming into existence is made contingent here on the presence of an entity that is finite (i.e., the human entity), would it not necessarily follow that it too must be a finite entity? And if this be the case, would this not undermine the arrogation of perfectibility and therefore of ultimacy to the divine entity here, thus undermining the very feasibility of its being an authentic divine entity, seeing that the notion of divinity in its very essence signifies ultimacy? Now clearly, the validity of the observations made here and the logical consistency of the inferences drawn from them cannot be denied. A divine entity constituting itself as a Thou entity is indeed dependent for its coming into existence and sustaining itself within it on the corresponding presence of a human entity (i.e., of another Thou entity), and seeing that the world for the largest part of its existence was indeed devoid of the presence of the human entity, it should follow, therefore, according to our analysis here, that the world must have existed for a long time without the possibility of a divine entity constituting itself as a Thou entity coming into existence or sustaining itself within it.

Clearly, the foregoing analysis implicates a most fundamental and serious problem with respect to the availability of a divine entity which constitutes itself as a pure Thou entity inasmuch as it challenges the very feasibility of a Thou-God coming into existence and/or sustaining itself within it without at the same time, as a result of this, inevitably compromising its perfectibility and as such its ultimacy which is, as we have seen, tantamount to saying without abdicating its status of being an entity that is authentically divine. For in not being ultimate it cannot be an authentic divine entity, seeing that the very essence of the authentic notion of divinity lies, as we have tried to show, in its being ultimate. Thus, if the foregoing analysis is valid, it indeed must precipitate a most serious problem.

It would seem to us, however, that upon closer examination the problem here could be decidedly overcome. For the attribute which is implicated here as the factor responsible for undermining the validity of the notion of divinity, to wit, the attribute of finitude, is an attribute that can arise only in the context of the It-dimension. This is so inasmuch as the It-dimension is a dimension that constitutes itself in terms of power and as such it is a dimension which implicates quantification (i.e., more and less of power) and existence in the flux thus implicating, in turn, a coming into and going out of existence for all penultimate entities that constitute themselves in its terms. And this being the case, in order for the divine entity to safeguard the authenticity of its divinity, it must preclude finitude in any of its possible expressions but most significantly it must preclude finitude as it expresses itself in terms of power and in terms of temporality—it cannot possess less than infinite power and infinite duration of existence within the flux. If it does (as is the case regarding the divine entity implicated in the foregoing analysis where it is viewed as being dependent on another entity, thus manifesting finitude in terms of power, and as being inextricably linked to that other entity, i.e., the human entity, it being finite in the duration of is existence, thus manifesting finitude in terms of duration), then it cannot be taken as being authentically divine, seeing that as such it cannot validly claim ultimacy. But, while the conclusion of the analysis above would admittedly apply to an It-God, i.e., to an entity constituting itself as ultimate in the context of the It-dimension, it cannot apply to a Thou-God, i.e., to an entity that constitutes itself as ultimate in the context of the Thou-dimension, a dimension that constitutes itself in terms of consciousness rather than in terms of power, and as such a dimension that does not lend itself to quantification or to existence in the flux, thus precluding these factors from undermining ultimacy in the context of this dimension. Indeed, finitude either with respect to duration or with respect to power cannot apply here, seeing that a Thou entity does not exist in the flux nor does it constitute itself in terms of power. If anything, dependency, here far from undermining any possibility of arrogating ultimacy to an entity, is an inextricable and essential attribute of every Thou entity, seeing that it underlies the very feasibility of its coming into existence and sustaining itself in it.

Indeed, the notion of ultimacy in the context of the Thou-dimension formulates itself not in terms of infinitude but in terms of exclusivity—a Thou entity is ultimate when it constitutes itself exclusively in the context of the Thou-dimension. Thus, unlike the situation with respect to an It-God where finitude does indeed undermine the arrogation of ultimacy and therefore also of the status of divinity, with respect to a Thou-God it does not. The analysis above clearly goes astray in applying an evaluation that formulates itself in the context of the It-dimension to any entity that constitutes itself exclusively in the context of the Thou-dimension.

That such a going astray in the above analysis was possible in the first place is most probably due to the fact that the above analysis, only naturally and indeed inescapably, grounds itself in the perspective of the human entity and that this perspective—seeing that it encompasses both the It-dimension and the Thou-dimension inasmuch as the human entity constitutes itself in terms of both these dimensions—lends itself to the invalid mixing of elements from both dimensions. Indeed, such a mixing is almost unavoidable, seeing that the Thou-dimension can be made available to the human entity only through its "refraction" in the It-dimension, which is to say, only through its bending within the flux of time. Only in such a context could the question arise as to how could the divine entity come into existence or be within it prior to the human entity being in existence. In the context of the Thou-dimension, when taken exclusively in its own terms, this question does not make sense—the pure Thou entity, by its very essence, can neither come into existence nor exit from existence. The Thou-entity by its very essence subsists in eternity, which is to say, outside the flow of time. Thus, from the vantage point of the Thou-dimension taken exclusively in its own terms, the question here is based on a misconception of what is and what is not feasible in the context of the Thou-dimension and as such it is beside the point and of no consequence.[18]

Thus, having a divine entity that ontologically constitutes itself exclusively in terms of the dimension-of-consciousness, i.e., that ontologically constitutes itself as a pure Thou entity, does in no way weaken, leave alone undermine, the religious relevancy or efficacy of the divine entity (and, of course, commensurate to this, it in no way weakens or undermines the relevancy or meaningfulness of any religion that formulates itself within the context of the dimension-of-consciousness). The divine entity does not need to possess power in order to be an efficacious agent, i.e., in order to play a relevant and meaningful role in the economy of redemption/salvation. And this being the case, the innovative and, indeed, revolutionary religious formulation introduced within the Hebrew bible by the prophetic strand did not have to retain the arrogation of power to its divine entity. It could have given it up altogether and proceed all the way to offer us a divine entity that is completely devoid of power, a pure Thou-God, without in any way compromising its efficacy and relevancy (and, indeed, as an added all-important bonus avoid *ab initio* the highly problematic issue of theodicy).

Notes

1. Of course, it may be objected that the real, essential distinction of these religions, i.e., of pagan religions, lies in their being polytheistic rather than monotheistic (in the

arithmetic sense) and not in formulating themselves in relation to an It-god. For one may well point to the divine entities encountered in these religions, i.e., to the divine entities populating their polytheistic pantheons, to the effect that they are after all personal entities and thus Thou-gods, not It-gods. But this objection can be disposed of quite readily on two grounds. First, the divine entities encountered in the pantheons of these religions are not entities that are ultimate. Indeed, it is precisely because they are not ultimate that these religions can be polytheistic (ultimacy by definition must be unitary—it cannot countenance multiplicity). True, the divine entities in polytheistic religions are more powerful than humans, but they are not all-powerful; in the last analysis, they are but "man writ large." These divine entities too, like humans, are subjected to a more powerful entity lying beyond them (be it Moira in Greek religion or Fatum in Roman religion or Maat in Egyptian religion) and it is this entity which is the ultimate entity and as such the authentic divine entity; and, this entity is constituted in terms of blind power. (We may note in passing that some early tribal religions do not formulate themselves in relation to an ultimate entity but are content to stop short in formulating themselves in relation to an entity that is penultimate, an entity that is more powerful than the human but is not all-powerful. In a way, this is quite understandable, seeing that the drive to relate to an entity that is ultimate may be motivated more by abstract metaphysical concerns than by practical needs and that in primitive circumstances of existence, which after all are the circumstances characterizing the existence of such early tribal religions, it is the practical and not the metaphysical which characterizes the needs of the community—in primitive circumstances of existence all that the human is likely to expect and hope for is help from an entity more powerful than itself but not necessarily omnipotent. But even so they too are pagan religions, i.e., religions that constitute themselves in the context of the dimension-of-power inasmuch as their relations to their penultimate gods are I-It relations, i.e., relations of utilization in terms of power.)

Secondly, even aside from the consideration that the polytheistic divine entities are not ultimate but only penultimate entities, we have the further consideration that these divine entities are not really personal entities after all. In their essence they are manifestations of the forces of nature and as such they constitute themselves in terms of the dimension-of-power, as It entities, and not in terms of the dimension-of-consciousness, as Thou entities. They appear as personal entities by virtue of their being personified by us, namely, because we relate to them as if they were personal entities ascribing to them personal attributes (in a similar way to the personification that some of us may endow a pet animal with or even a favorite car or boat). Clearly, this impinges upon the way we perceive them and relate to them but it does not change what they are in reality, to wit, entities constituted in terms of the dimension-of-power. Indeed, even though we personify them, which is to say, see them as personal entities endowed with the capacities to will, think, and feel like humans, the underlying relation both from the humans to them and from them to the humans is nonetheless exclusively in terms of power, very much an I-It relation, seeing that it is essentially a relation of mutual utilization, a relation of a *quid pro quo* exchange of power.

Thus, we must conclude that the possible objection cited here is not, in the last analysis, valid and that, therefore, the fundamental division within the history of religion is not between religions that relate to a plurality of penultimate divine entities and religions that relate to a single divine penultimate entity (as is the case, for example, in henotheism and monolatery) but rather, as we claimed above, between religions relating to a divine entity *qua* the ultimate entity (thus, of necessity a single entity) that constitutes itself in terms of blind power and religions relating to such a divine entity but one that constitutes itself in terms of personhood.

2. Granted, the case made here for this claim based itself exclusively on the ontological constitution of the entity that authentically represents the divine in these religions, namely, the entity representing ultimacy in the context of the dimension-of-power, and did not pursue the various other characterizations that are connected with religions that constitute themselves in the context of the dimension-of-power and which can be encountered in pagan religions such as sanctification of space rather than of time (to wit, encountering the divine in nature rather than in history), a hierarchical gradation in the presence of holiness, the format of worship expressing itself in action rather than in words, and in incorporating magic and divination rather than address, in short, in being a relating to the divine in terms of utilization rather than of affirmation. But given our claim that the ontological constitution of the divine entity (in its authentic sense) is the defining characterization of the kind of religion implicated, the case made here only in terms of the ontological constitution of the divine entity should suffice, seeing that it establishes the claim in a fundamental, albeit minimalist, manner. In any event, some of these supplemental characterizations will be discussed below.

3. Indeed, as such, these three concrete historical expressions of religion are usually referred to as the biblical or Abrahamic religions. We adopt this term but we use it primarily not to denote the three particular concrete historical religions as such but rather to denote that which constitutes their common denominator, that being their belonging to the type of religion that grounds itself in the dimension-of-consciousness, in the same way that we primarily use the term pagan religion to denote not the various non-biblical religions but rather that which constitutes their common-denominator, namely, their belonging to the type of religion that grounds itself in the dimension-of-power.

4. By the way, these two strands are not to be confused with the four sources introduced by the documentary hypothesis though some connection and, indeed, overlapping may be established between them. This is so inasmuch as the division between the priestly and the prophetic strands is based on theological differences in the religious formulation reflected in the text while the division in the documentary hypothesis is based on differences in the literary composition of the text such as differences in style, vocabulary and historical or geographical references, the former giving us a division with respect to the kind of religious structure implicated in the text while the latter giving us a division with respect to the authorship of the text. Still inasmuch as the text here inescapably implicates also a theological orientation, the division in the documentary hypothesis may well include also a difference in the theological orientation of the text and to that extent an overlap between the two divisions may well be feasible. Indeed, as such, an overlap between the priestly strand and the P and E sources in the documentary hypothesis, on the one hand, and the prophetic strand and the D and J sources in the documentary hypothesis, on the other hand, may perhaps suggest itself. Lastly, in consequence of the foregoing consideration, one further difference between the documentary hypothesis, on the one hand, and specifically the prophetic strand, on the other, may suggest itself in that the documentary hypothesis (and here also the priestly strand, seeing that it identifies itself with the P source in the documentary hypothesis) applies primarily to the pentatench (thus, in the main, to the legal corpora and the mythological remnants in the text) while the prophetic strand applies primarily to the prophetic books and the historical narrative in the text.

5. Henotheism and monolatery signify in essence the same thing, except that henotheism expresses it with respect to the metaphysical status of the divine entity, i.e., in theory, while monolatery expresses it with respect to the mode of relating to the divine entity, i.e., in praxis. Thus, in the henotheistic formulation, a community of faith recognizes the existence of a single divine entity but, in principle, does not negate the validity

of other communities of faith recognizing the existence of other divine entities, while in the formulation of monolatery, a community of faith confines its worship to a single divine entity but, in principle, does not deny the efficacy of the worship of other divine entities in other communities of faith.

6. True, there have been accusations mainly leveled against Christianity (from the Jewish and Moslem side) regarding its doctrine of the Trinity, but also against Halachic Judaism and Islam particularly with respect to their mystical expressions, namely, the Kabbalah and Sufism respectively, that they all compromise the oneness of the divine entity by introducing additional divine entities. But although on the surface these accusations may seem plausible, a more careful examination would not, in the last analysis, sustain them. Thus, turning to the doctrine of the Trinity in Christianity, which is after all the main object of the criticism, it should be noted that mainstream, "official" Christianity always insisted that the doctrine of the Trinity did not implicate the existence of three distinct, separate entities, thus a plurality of divine entities, but rather the existence of one, single divine entity which manifests itself in three different forms, three different *persona*. Thus, threesome does not refer to a plurality of entities (beings) but rather to a plurality of forms manifested by one, single entity. And, by the way, the fact that this signification given to the doctrine in "official" Christianity is for many people rationally incomprehensible (indeed many Christian theologians have through the ages owned up to the fact that the doctrine when taken in the "official" signification is ultimately a mystery) has really no bearing on the point we are making here. For what matters is that "official" Christianity adheres to the doctrine only in the signification delineated here. Indeed, "official" Christianity rejected as heretical—as, for example, was the case with Arianism—any interpretation of the Trinity which implied that we have a number of different, distinct entities, particularly when the implication was that the father and the son were two distinct, separate entities, and this signification, irrespective of the fact that rationally it may be incomprehensible, clearly rejects a multiplicity of divine entities and consequently in principle must preclude the possibility of adopting a henotheistic or a monolaterist stance.

Finally, to round off the discussion here, the point can also be made that a similar formulation to that encountered in the doctrine of the Trinity, i.e., a formulation that seems to implicate a breakdown of the oneness of the divine entity into a number of distinct, separate divine entities, can also be encountered in Halachic Judaism and Islam, though in these religious traditions it is not nearly as central or foundational in their respective religious structures as is the doctrine of the Trinity within the religious structure of Christianity. In Halachic Judaism and in Islam such a formulation finds expression more peripherally, to wit, in their respective mystical expressions. Thus, to give one example, in the Kabbalah, in addition to encountering the divine entity as the *Ein Sof*, i.e., the transcendent infinite divine entity, one can also encounter the divine entity as the *Schechinah*, i.e., the indwelling, the immanent divine entity, and indeed also as the ten *sefirot*, the ten spheres through which the *Ein Sof* emanates itself and thus, in so doing, constituting the world. But these different encounters of the divine entity do not implicate, by and large, for the kabbalists a compromising of the oneness of the divine entity (and this is so, even though we have a gender differentiation here, seeing that the *Ein Sof* is a masculine term while the *Schechinah* is feminine term).

7. The inference implied here that because the divine entity here is ultimate, the power arrogated to it must also per force be ultimate (which with regard to the notion of power means infinite) would seem to us, however, to be invalid. It would have been valid had the divine entity and the power arrogated to it been formulated in the context of the same dimension. But this is evidently not the case here. We and, for that matter, all the

various expressions of biblical religion (i.e., classical biblical prophecy, Halachic Judaism, Christianity, Islam) accept this inference as almost self-evident because we neglect to factor in the fact that here the entity and the attribute/capacity arrogated to it constitute themselves in the context of two different dimensions. Overlooking this fact, it would indeed seem only natural to assume that all the attributes/capacities possessed by an entity that is ultimate will themselves also be per force ultimate. But as argued here, this should not apply if the entity and certain attributes/capacities arrogated to it constitute themselves in the context of two different dimensions. Indeed, if the entity and these attributes/capacities arrogated to it constitute themselves in two different dimensions, it should be quite feasible for the entity to be ultimate in the context of its dimension and for these attributes/capacities arrogated to it to be penultimate in the context of their dimension. Thus, a divine entity constituting itself as an ultimate entity in the dimension-of-consciousness can have finite power arrogated to it.

Of course, by arrogating infinite power to an entity that constitutes itself as ultimate, i.e., as divine, in the context of the dimension-of-consciousness, the various expressions of biblical religion end up with a divine entity that is simultaneously ultimate in the context of two dimensions, namely, in the context of the dimension-of-consciousness and in the context of the dimensions-of-power. Now, in principle and in its own terms, this too should be feasible. An entity should be able to be simultaneously ultimate in two or more different dimensions (and how much more so, if the entity is penultimate in the two or more dimensions involved). Indeed the only configuration that in principle should not be feasible here is to have simultaneously two entities as ultimate entities in the context of one and the same dimension.

We can perhaps better appreciate the rationale underlying our claims here if we briefly consider the parallel scenarios that are possible with respect to another relation that can be seen, we would submit, as analogous to the relation under consideration here, i.e., the relation between the notion of ultimacy and the notion of dimension, this being the relation between the notion of kingship and the notion of country, the former notion being analogous to the notion of ultimacy and the latter notion being analogous to the notion of dimension. Thus, it is feasible (and indeed we have any number of concrete historical examples of this) for one and the same person (i.e., one and the same entity) to be at one and the same time a reigning monarch in two or more different countries—see, for example, the reigning monarchs from the house of Windsor being kings simultaneously of great Britain and of the various previous dominions, or the reigning monarchs from the house of Hapsburg being simultaneously emperors of Austria and kings of Hungary. (By the way, through this mechanism different countries can be united into a kind of one entity, e.g., the British Commonwealth or the Austrian-Hungarian Empire, and this can serve as a useful argument at the disposal of monotheistic religious formulations by which to overcome Gnostic dualism in the face of the ontological bifurcation of reality between the dimension-of-power and the dimension-of-consciousness; namely, these two dimensions which are not reducible to each other do not have to necessarily implicate two divine entities, e.g., the god of love or light and the god of wrath or darkness, but rather can still implicate only a single entity that would be ultimate in the context of both). Likewise, it may be feasible for an individual who is not a king to be simultaneously a subject in two or more countries. Lastly, it is also feasible (though, granted, it may be perhaps less readily evident) that one and the same individual can be at the same time a king in one country and something less than a king, e.g., a prince or a duke, in another country—see, for example, the various German princes who were also kings in some of the Balkan countries or, for that matter, the Hanoverian princes in the 18th century who were also kings of Great Britain.

Still valid or interesting as these considerations may or may not be, they are, in the last analysis, beside the point as far as what is specifically under consideration here, to wit, the issue of what are the possible parameters of the power arrogated to an entity constituting itself as ultimate in the context of the dimension-of-consciousness. For as we shall presently try to argue, the very arrogation of power to an entity constituting itself as ultimate in the context of the dimension-of-consciousness is, because of some further consideration, not feasible to begin with.

8. The serious problematic which the arrogation of infinite power to the divine entity precipitates for biblical religion (particularly as regards its expression in the prophetic strand and in Halachic Judaism where the focus is on the attribute of justice seeing it as constituting the very essence of the function of the divine in the structure of the religious phenomenon) is the problematic of theodicy, i.e., the problematic of justifying the divine entity in the face of the existence of evil in its implication of injustice (evil, of course, implicates also suffering and in this sense its existence would precipitate the problematic of theodicy with respect to all those religious formulations which focus on the attribute of goodness in the divine entity). For clearly, if the divine entity is just and, at the same time, is all-powerful, then the existence of injustice would per force precipitate the problematic of theodicy. And the only feasible way of overcoming the problematic of theodicy, i.e., of exonerating the divine entity, in these circumstances (seeing that the attribute of justice constitutes the very essence of the divine entity in biblical religion and consequently the abrogation of this attribute would necessarily signify the dissolution of biblical religion), is by abrogating the arrogation of infinite power, of omnipotence, to the divine entity.

Still, the various religious traditions that formulate themselves within the context of biblical religion tend, nonetheless, to reject the possibility of abrogating the arrogation of omnipotence to the divine entity. The rationale underlying this rejection seems to be quite clear—the fact that the divine entity here is an entity that is ultimate necessarily implicates that all attributes arrogated to it must also, in their terms, be ultimate and therefore with respect to the attribution of power it must be the attribution of infinite power. Thus, indeed, there are three strategies purporting to overcome the problematic of theodicy that have considerable long-standing currency in the various religious traditions that formulate themselves in the context of biblical religion, all of them proposing the overcoming of the problematic of theodicy while retaining the arrogation of omnipotence to the divine entity. We have the strategy first offered by the friends in the book of Job in which the omnipotence of God is left intact while at the same time the justice of this God is supposedly exonerated (and this in the face of the suffering meted out by Him to innocent people) by maintaining that the innocence of such people is misleading and that in truth they must have sinned and indeed sinned commensurately with the suffering meted out to them. Similarly, we have the strategy, also first presented in the book of Job, that, again, while holding firmly to the arrogation of omnipotence to God, admits that its reconciliation with the arrogation of justice to God in the face of what is happening in our world is a mystery that transcends the capacity of human understanding but that this does not in any way mean to say that no reconciliation is available—from God's vantage point there is full exoneration and justification of His justice in the way He runs the world. Lastly, we have the strategy held by quite a few religious thinkers across the board, which while, like the foregoing two strategies, insists on arrogating omnipotence to God, suggests at the same time that God out of His own free will opts to restrict the deployment of His omnipotence, thus leaving room for human activity and thus for the perpetration of evil without thereby compromising His justice.

But clearly, none of these three strategies is persuasive. Regarding the strategy mentioned here first, it clearly flies in the face of our experience—while our experience clearly shows the individual to be innocent, it maintained that the individual has sinned. Indeed, even the Jobian God who was to be a beneficiary of this strategy rejects it in no uncertain terms—and rightly so! And as regards the second strategy presented here, it is tantamount to admitting bankruptcy. For the very point of our undertaking here is to overcome the problematic of theodicy in a manner that would be rationally persuasive and this strategy clearly admits that it cannot provide us with such a rationality—it rejects the very possibility of providing it. Now, resorting to mystery may be acceptable in the context of faith, i.e., when things are to be undertaken on faith, but not in the context of attempting to grasp things rationally. Lastly, as regards the third strategy, since no persuasive reason is given as to why the divine entity would freely opt to limit the deployment of the infinite power that is at its disposal, one cannot escape the suspicion that it smacks of being a *deus ex machina* strategy. For what is the point of arrogating omnipotence to an entity if its deployment is to be limited on a permanent basis? Indeed, does it make any sense to claim on behalf of an entity that it possesses omnipotence when the power it will ever exercise will in fact always remain limited? If the power exercised by an entity is in reality always limited, then can we really meaningfully say that such an entity possesses omnipotence? Is it not for all intents and purposes in possession of limited power? Finally, and perhaps most damaging, one cannot escape the question that if God is in possession of infinite power and He freely opts not to deploy it in order to prevent horrific acts of evil from occurring, can He really be exonerated from responsibility for the occurrence of such acts?

Indeed, more recently (and perhaps, at least partially, in response to the fact that previous formulations were deemed unsatisfactory) we can encounter an alternative formulation (for example, in process theology) that gives up on insisting on arrogating omnipotence to the divine entity and grants up front that the power at the disposal of the divine entity, at least till now, has been finite. Now it cannot be denied that this strategy would clearly dispose of the problematic of theodicy. Nonetheless, and notwithstanding the considerable advantage that such a disposal would afford, this strategy may prove to many unacceptable on the ground that it undermines the ultimacy of the divine entity inasmuch as it may be contended that an ultimate entity cannot be arrogated a penultimate attribute. Thus, if a divine entity were to possess power it would have to possess infinite power. However, in view of the stance we have taken above (albeit somewhat hesitatingly) whereby it should be possible for one and the same entity to be ultimate in the context of one dimension and penultimate in the context of another dimension, we clearly cannot readily adopt this line of criticism. Still, in the last analysis, we too cannot accept this strategy but because of a different consideration, a consideration that we would presently address below.

9. Indeed, paganism in encountering the ultimate as blind power is at one with the perspective/orientation of secularism as it expresses itself, for example, in the enterprises of philosophy and of science. In the last analysis, they are, at bottom, one and the same, seeing that the ultimate "stuff" in terms of which the sum total of reality constitutes itself is the same for both—for both it is blind power. Indeed, this ultimate at-oneness between the perspective/orientation of secularism and that of paganism manifests itself in the fact that a transition from the latter to the former is readily feasible as can be actually observed in the history of Ancient Greece when, on the one hand, the mythologic expression of paganism readily lent itself to being transformed into the philosophic enterprise and, on the other hand, its rites of magic and divination readily lent themselves to being transformed into the enterprise of science. In the last analysis, the distinction between the

perspective/orientation of paganism and that of secularism is, so to speak, merely a quantitative but not a qualitative distinction, a distinction merely in degree (i.e., in the degree of the validity of the knowledge of the reality that lies beyond us and commensurately in the degree of the reliability of the predictions that can be made on its basis) but not in substance (i.e., in terms of the kind of ultimate "stuff" in terms of which that reality constitutes itself)—the religious expression of paganism is merely a more primitive stage (in the sense of resorting to imagination and to concrete picturing rather than to rational inference and abstract thinking) in the human endeavor to authentically grasp the nature and working of reality and consequently to better reap the benefits emanating from such a grasp than is the philosophical/scientific expression of secularism.

So, when one refers to the distinction between the secularist and the religious perspective/orientation, this applies, strictly speaking, to the religious perspective/orientation as it expresses itself in biblical religion but not as it expresses itself in pagan religion (by the way, in the Hebrew bible, particularly in its prophetic strand, there is no transition to philosophy or to science—neither finds expression in this context). Indeed, the religious perspective/orientation as it expresses itself in pagan religion belongs, in the last analysis, on the side of the perspective/orientation of secularism. Thus the fundamental bifurcation which confronts us is, therefore, the bifurcation between secularism and paganism on the one hand and biblical religion on the other, the former grounding themselves in the dimension-of-power, i.e., encountering the ultimate as blind power, while the latter grounds itself in the dimension-of-consciousness, i.e., encountering the ultimate as a person (by the way, it may be interesting to note that pagan religion, but clearly not biblical religion, readily lends itself to being referred to in terms of an "ism", i.e., paganism, in the same way that the secular perspective/orientation readily lends itself to being referred to in terms of an "ism", i.e., secularism).

Finally, we should briefly point out that from this fundamental bifurcation between being grounded in blind power and being grounded in consciousness, i.e., in personhood, any number of further distinctions that are particularly of great significance with respect to the domain of religion, arise. These distinctions can be clearly traced to the fact that power by its very essence constitutes itself as an unbroken, uninterrupted continuum tolerating no "gaps," no over-againstness, while consciousness, personhood, by its very essence can constitute itself only in the context of an over-againstness, namely, in placing itself (or, even more accurately, in finding itself placed) over-against an other. Thus, for example, it should be readily understandable in light of this observation why pagan religion does, in the last analysis, always lend itself to a pantheistic formulation while biblical religion must, by its very essence, reject any formulation of itself that smacks of pantheism and insist uncompromisingly that it can lend itself only to a theistic formulation; or why in pagan religion the enterprise of theology readily lends itself to being pursued through the approach of natural theology (namely, the approach whereby the discourse regarding the divine entity, e.g., the discourse attempting to establish its existence and describe its attributes, grounds itself in inferences drawn from the world as experienced by us) while in biblical religion such an approach is, in the last analysis, not feasible and the theological enterprise must instead be pursued through the approach of revelatory theology (namely, the approach whereby any and all discourse regarding the divine entity—the discourse here centering on the relating of the divine entity to the human, e.g., its demands of and promises to the human, rather than on proving its existence or describing its attributes—grounds itself in the self-disclosure of the divine entity).

10. Indeed, a good case can be made that it is not only a matter of can but that, for all intents and purposes, it is the only way in which the predicament and the overcoming of the predicament can be formulated when their formulation is with respect to power.

With respect to power, their formulation has to remain within the parameters of finite power, a formulation of the predicament in terms of not enough power and of the overcoming of the predicament in terms of increased power—there can be no viable formulation of the predicament in terms of the total absence of power and of the overcoming in terms of the possession of infinite power. For formulating the predicament in terms of the total absence of power would preclude the very possibility of existence for the human or, for that matter, for any other conceivable entity within the dimension-of-power capable of bearing a predicament. And formulating the overcoming in terms of the possession of infinite power would likewise preclude the possibility of existence for any particular individual entity (including, of course, any particular individual human entity), seeing that it would necessarily implicate the inclusion of the sum total of all existent entities within the redeemed entity and thus, in turn, necessarily implicating the cancellation of its individuality. In other words, saying that an individual entity is arrogated infinite power is tantamount to saying that it is totally absorbed, swallowed, within the entity that encompasses the sum total of all existent entities (this being, by the way, the redeemed state of affairs which the formulation of mysticism envisions and which as such is a very telling indicator that the phenomenon of mysticism formulates itself in the context of the dimension-of-power).

11. By the way, the psychological need is most likely to arise in the earlier, more primitive stages of human development and progressively dissipate as human development advances. We should expect therefore to encounter personification, the hallmark of the religious formulation of paganism, in the "childhood" stages of humanity and its transformation, as humanity matures, into the acceptance of the impersonal reality of blind power as this manifests itself in the rationalist secularism of science and philosophy. Indeed, as noted above, this can be seen, for example, in the transformation in classical Greece from the presentation of blind power in the context of myth to its presentation in the context of metaphysics and in the transformation in the relating to it from magic/divination to science.

12. Some would, no doubt, want to challenge this assertion by claiming that in the human we may encounter instances in which consciousness manifests itself in degree (e.g., states of semi- or borderline consciousness). To this we may reply that such claims are based exclusively on the impressions of the observer (impressions that are far from being clear and certain, indeed, impressions that are really more in the way of being suspicions and wishful thinking) and are in no way substantiated by the subject. Indeed, at the time of occurrence the subject does not respond and subsequently has no recollection. But even if one could firmly establish that states of borderline consciousness do occur in the human, this can be accounted for by the fact that consciousness in the human must inescapably be mediated through the mechanism of the body (an entity that belongs to the dimension-of-power) and it is by virtue of this that consciousness here can be refracted into degrees of partial consciousness. However, consciousness in its own terms cannot be so refracted.

13. Indeed, the divine entity here becomes in its ontological constitution identical with the pantheonic divine entities of pagan religion except that they are only given more power than the human, (namely, they are given increased power compared to the power given to the human but still a degree of power that remains within the boundaries of the finite) while it is given infinite power—the difference here is merely quantitative. Both are but "man writ large," except that with respect to the pantheonic divine entities it is but a case of "man writ larger" while with respect to the divine entity of the concrete, historical expressions of biblical religion it is a case of "man writ largest."

14. True, the themes of creation and providence (and the implication of the divine entity in both) are very central and widely held in all three concrete, historical expressions of biblical religion. This, of course, is a reflection of the inextricable placement of the human within the dimension-of-power and in consequence of this of his/her need in this context to implicate an entity that possesses a considerable measure of greater power in order to account for the world coming into existence and for the way it is run (and even more to the point, to serve as a source of help to the human in his/her coping with the hardships that such a world is likely to pose to him/her). Still, a good case can be made that negating the implication of the divine entity in these two themes, i.e, in the theme of creation and in that of providence, and thus entailing their collapse, would not undermine the viability of any of the concrete, historical expressions of biblical religion (with the possible exception of Islam).

Thus, as the noted Old Testament theologian von Rad asserted, the phenomenon of biblical religion, i.e., the distinctive faith that finds expression in the Hebrew Bible, has its beginning not in the event of creation (an event brought about by an act carried out with respect to nature, namely, in the context of space) but in the event of the exodus from Egypt (an event brought about by an act carried out with respect to history, namely, in the context of time). Indeed, it is very doubtful if the distinctive faith coming into expression in the Hebrew Bible, i.e., the prophetic strand of biblical religion, would have been significantly affected had the material contained in the book of Genesis never been included within the Hebrew Bible. Certainly, one may well argue that this material reflects the beliefs, customs and ways of life characterizing the religious orientation of ancient Mesopotamia (a religious orientation that squarely grounds itself in pagan religion) rather than the distinctive religious orientation of the Hebrew bible, and that in consequence of this, while the material contained in the book of Genesis may well be of great value to the scholar interested in the religions and civilizations of the Ancient Near East, it is not particularly of great value to the scholar interested in the distinctive religious orientation of the Hebrew bible. But aside from this and, indeed, much more significantly, is the fact that the notion of creation, in its very essence, comes to address a scientific concern in that it comes to give an account of how the world as we know it has come into existence (and as such it belongs to the same class of accounts as that given by the big bang theory of contemporary physics or that given by the Darwinian evolutionary theory in biology). Indeed, the notion of creation is embraced and given such prominent attention within the respective formulations of the various concrete, historical expressions of pagan religion precisely because pagan religion formulates itself in the context of the dimension-of-power, namely because it formulates itself in the same dimension in which the enterprise of science formulates itself (and as such also it should not be surprising that, in the last analysis, pagan religion readily lends itself to being reducible to science, that it is in effect a form of "primitive science"—science in terms of what its concerns are and primitive in the way it attempts to cope with them and consequently in the results it attains). But the distinctiveness of biblical religion lies precisely in the fact that it formulates itself not in the context of the dimension-of-power but in the context of the dimension-of-consciousness and as such it, in contradistinction to pagan religion, does not lend itself to being reducible to the enterprise of science (indeed, if anything, it lends itself to being reducible to the enterprise of ethics so that, by the way, the mode of secularization here would not be via the reduction of religion to science, as is the case with pagan religion, but rather via the reduction of religion to ethics). And this, of course, means that the concerns of science, such as the concern with how the world has come into existence or with how it has come to be constituted the way it is (concerns which clearly implicate the notion of creation), are not concerns which biblical religion would address.

And as regards the notion of providence, a good case can be made that not only does this notion address a concern that is very much a concern of science and not of biblical religion, to wit, a concern that impinges upon the issue of how the world is being run, and that, therefore, its abrogation should in no way affect the viability of biblical religion, but rather, that its abrogation, if anything, would actually provide a most significant bonus to biblical religion. For as we had occasion to argue in a different publication (see my essay "Divine Providence in the Context of Judaism" in *God Commands*, vol. 2, edited by J. Neusner, Mercer University Press, 1995), the notion of providence inescapably precipitates the problematic of theodicy, a problematic that is most fundamental and troublesome for biblical religion (indeed, a problematic that impinges upon the very essence of biblical religion), and the only way in which this problematic can be validly overcome is by divesting the divine entity of all power so that it cannot be implicated in the running of the world. The alternative strategy by which the problematic of theodicy is to be overcome put forth by process theology, the strategy whereby the divine entity is to be left in possession of finite and no longer infinite power, is really, as we have already had occasion to note, not viable even though it is admittedly effective in overcoming the problematic of theodicy. This is so because, as we have pointed out, inasmuch as it precludes the power arrogated to the divine entity from being infinite, it necessarily undermines the ultimacy of the divine entity and as such it undermines the very signification of the authentic notion of divinity. An entity that is not ultimate cannot be an authentic divine entity. Yes, the strategy put forth by process theology succeeds in throwing out the dirty water (i.e., overcoming the problematic of theodicy) but it can do that only at the cost of throwing out the baby with the dirty water (i.e. precluding the presence of an authentic divine entity).

Of course, it can be argued that inasmuch as the ultimacy of the divine entity is undermined here only with regard to its ultimacy within the context of the dimension-of-power but not with regard to its ultimacy within the context of the dimension-of-consciousness, such undermining when directed to biblical religion is beside the point—it misses the mark. Now, this objection may indeed appear valid if it is taken only as far as it goes. But it can nonetheless be readily undermined by pointing out that if the divine entity with which we are dealing here is an ultimate entity exclusively within the context of the dimension-of-consciousness, then, as we already argued above, no power whatsoever, leave alone infinite power, can be arrogated to it.

Thus, inasmuch as the problematic of theodicy may well jeopardize the viability of biblical religion and in view of the fact that the problematic of theodicy can be overcome only through the abrogation of the notion of providence, the abrogation of the notion of providence must be seen not as an act that undermines the viability of biblical religion but, just the opposite, as an act that rescues the viability of biblical religion.

15. By the way, this would mean, of course, that in such a delineation of the ethical enterprise the enterprise can be meaningfully applicable only with respect to human entities, seeing that in contradistinction to the entities of nature and to the divine entity, both of these kinds of entities constituting themselves exclusively in terms of only one of these two dimensions (the former constituting themselves exclusively in terms of the It-dimension and the latter constituting itself exclusively in terms of the Thou-dimension), the human entity is the only entity that constitutes itself in terms of both the It-dimension and the Thou-dimension, being constituted as an inextricable It/Thou entity (of course, if a persuasive case can be made with respect to entities belonging to certain species of the animal kingdom that such entities do also constitute themselves in terms of both the It-dimension and the Thou-dimension, then the enterprise of ethics would clearly be applicable to them too).

16. Given our depiction here of the entity constituting itself as a Thou as being dependent on a source outside itself to extend to it affirmation, it would seem that the appellation of a being-by-another rather than a being-for-another would be more appropriate. Actually, a more detailed analysis of the process by which affirmation is extended and received (as we have tried to do in another place) will show that both appellations, that of being a being-for-another and that of being a being-by-another, are valid, seeing that the process implicates simultaneously in one and the same act both a giving and a receiving of affirmation. A Thou-being is at one and the same time a being-for-another in that it cannot but extend affirmation and a being-by-another in that it cannot but be dependent on affirmation being extended to it. The appellation of being-for-another has become the appellation commonly used for a Thou-being and this is amply justified by the fact that the extension of affirmation is an essential and inextricable aspect of the Thou-being. We coined and introduced here the rather awkward appellation of being-by-another inasmuch as it seems to us to convey more precisely what is at stake in our analysis here, which is that our analysis here regarding the Thou-being focuses on its aspect of receiving rather than of extending affirmation.

17. True, regarding the feasibility of sustaining the human entity in existence, to the extent that it is constituted in terms of the Thou-dimension, and providing it with the possibility of establishing justice, one could perhaps argue that the fact that a great number of human entities are in existence at any given time may offset the negative prospects that arise regarding the affirmation being actually extended when its source is a fellow human entity, seeing that in such a context the source is contingent. For, given the large number of human entities in existence at any given time, the chances are that there would always be a human entity that would opt to extend affirmation. Still, in principle the possibility always remains that at any given time no human entity would opt to extend affirmation. Indeed, as noted above, the fact that the human entity constitutes itself not only in terms of the Thou-dimension but also in terms of the It-dimension gives it always the option to relate to its fellow human entity in terms of the It-dimension (i.e., in terms of utilization) and not in terms of the Thou-dimension (i.e., in terms of affirmation), thus making it, in the last analysis, an unreliable source for providing the needed affirmation.

18. There is one additional point that needs to be addressed here. Namely, granted that in the context of a Thou-dimension taken exclusively in its own terms the raising of the question would be based on a misconception and that therefore the challenge implied in it would be beside the point; this, however, is clearly not the case when the question is raised in the context of the human perspective, i.e., in a context that encompasses both the It- and the Thou-dimension. In this context raising the question is not illegitimate. Can we then overcome the challenge implied in the question? One possible response may well be the following. As we have argued above, in the human perspective the phenomenon of religion appears only with the coming into existence of the human entity which, in turn, clearly implicates that the coming into existence of the divine entity can be available in this perspective, i.e., in the human perspective, only in tandem with the coming into existence of the human entity. As such, this is the moment of the Beginning, the "big bang" event for the component of the Thou-dimension in the ontological constitution of the human entity in the same way as the physical big bang event is the beginning for the component of the It-dimension in the ontological constitution of the human entity. And as science claims from the vantage point of the It-dimension that what might have taken place before the physical big bang event is beyond our ken, beyond the legitimate borders of our "reality map," so too can biblical religion claim from the vantage point of the Thou-dimension that what might have taken place before its starting-point event is off our screen. Thus, what could have become a problem that would have undermined the

viability of our proposed move here to resort to a divine entity that is a pure Thou (i.e., that excludes altogether the dimension-of-power from its ontological constitution) is basically neutralized.

III

Halachic Judaism, Christianity and Islam— The Three "Daughter Religions" of the Hebrew Bible

But while, according to our argument here, the prophetic strand within the Hebrew bible could have given us a divine entity devoid of all power without in any way compromising its religious efficacy, the fact is that it did not. It gave us a divine entity, which is an authentic personal entity, an authentic Thou-God, who at the same time, however, possesses infinite power. This is what the Hebrew bible bequeaths to its three "daughter religions," all of them adopting it as the foundation on which they proceed to erect their respective religion formulations. As such, we encounter in biblical religion (i.e., the religious formulation encountered in the Hebrew bible and in its three "daughter religions") a divine entity which, in the last analysis, is not a pure Thou entity but an It/Thou entity, a divine entity whose ontological constitution is qualitatively the same as the ontological constitution of the human entity, the difference between the two being only quantitative. Thus, biblical religion retains in this respect the position of pagan religion with respect to their pantheonic gods in that it too gives us a divine entity that is but "man write large," except that in pagan religion the ontological constitution of the pantheonic gods remains in essence wholly within the dimension-of-power and the aspect of consciousness is incorporated merely as a personification rather than as a full-fledged personhood while in biblical religion the aspect of power that is added to the aspect of consciousness is a full-fledged authentic expression of the notion of power.

Now, while in all the religious formulations emanating from the Hebrew bible, namely, in the religious formulations of its three "daughter religions," power is being arrogated to the divine entity, the extent of the power actually arrogated differs considerably among these formulations. Thus, we would submit that a case can be made that in terms of the actual workings of power within these formulations (and not merely in terms of the theological declarations that the power arrogated is infinite, seeing that such declarations are forced upon the formulations here as foregone conclusions inasmuch as the power is arrogated here to an entity that is ultimate), it is in Islam that we encounter the most pronounced arrogation of power to the divine entity while in Halachic Judaism the arrogation is considerably mitigated and in Christianity the thrust of the inner logic of its formulation actually points to the abrogation of power as far as the divine entity is concerned.[1] And given our argument above that the way the divine entity is characterized in a religious formulation is a reliable reflection of the kind of formulation we are encountering, this, in turn means that the more pronounced the arrogation of power to the divine entity, the more predominant is the dimension-of-power (relative to the dimension-of-consciousness) as the dimension in terms of which the structure-of-faith formulates itself. And this being the case, our claim can be extended to state that in Islam the structure-of-faith formulates itself by and large in terms of the dimension-of-power (which, by the way, may perhaps account for Franz Rosenzweig relegating Islam to paganism), that in Judaism it formulates itself in terms of a more balanced proportionality between the dimension-of-power and the dimension-of-consciousness, and that in Christianity, when viewed in terms of its essential thrust, it formulates itself mainly in terms of the dimension-of-consciousness. Indeed, these three possibilities that arise when the religious structure formulates itself in terms of both the dimension-of-power and the dimension-of-consciousness find their concrete, historical expression in the three biblical "daughter-religions"—Halachic Judaism trying to maintain both dimensions in a more or less balanced form, Christianity tilting the balance towards the dimension-of-consciousness, and Islam tilting the balance towards the dimension-of-power. (By the way, from this vantage point one can view Islam and Christianity not only as "daughter religions" emanating from the religion of the Hebrew bible but as "daughter religions" emanating from Halachic Judaism, each emphasizing in the main only one of the two dimensions in terms of which the structure-of-faith of Halachic Judaism formulates itself, Islam emphasizing the dimension-of-power and Christianity emphasizing the dimension-of-consciousness. Put somewhat differently, it can also be said that Halachic Judaism can be seen as formulating itself essentially in terms of the dimension-of-consciousness emanating from the prophetic strand in the Hebrew Bible though at the same time hanging on to the dimension-of-power emanating from the priestly strand in the Hebrew Bible, while Islam, so to speak, retreats back to the dimension-of-power and Christianity advances towards the dimension-of-consciousness).

Now, to the extent that these claims would clearly require ultimately substantiation, the following observations may be advanced by way of providing some of this substantiation:

1) With respect to the naming of the divine entity, Islam uses a generic name signifying divinity, i.e., Allah; in Judaism, on the other hand, while the

generic name Eloha (or the plural name Elohim) can also be encountered (mainly in the priestly strand), a personal name, i.e., YHWH, is prominently present (indeed, exclusively so in the prophetic strand); and in Christianity with respect to the three manifestations of the divine, the manifestation which, religiously speaking, plays a central and indeed, for all intents and purposes, an exclusive role in its structure-of-faith, i.e., the second persona of the trinity, is accorded a full-fledged personal name, i.e., Jesus, and although it is true that the remaining two persona, i.e., the first and the third, are accorded names which are, strictly speaking, general and not personal ("Father" and "Holy Spirit"), the signification of these names clearly impinges on aspects that constitute the very essence of personhood, i.e., the aspects of fatherhood and spirit.

2) In Islam, the focus is almost exclusively on the might of the divine entity; in Judaism, on the other hand, while the might of the divine entity is certainly acknowledged, the focus is (again, principally in the prophetic strand) predominantly on the righteousness of the divine entity; and in Christianity the focus is clearly not on power (after all Jesus as the divine entity is devoid of all power) but rather on the unmerited love, i.e., agape, of the divine entity.

3) While, as already noted, the attributes of fatherhood and spirit are widely accorded to the divine entity in both Judaism and Christianity, they are totally absent in Islam.

4) In Islam, the focus is on the divine entity as creator, while in Judaism it is on the divine entity as redeemer and in Christianity it is on the divine entity as saviour (we distinguish between "redeemer" and "saviour", i.e., between "redemption" and "salvation," in that the former formulates itself in a this-worldly context while the latter formulates itself in an other-worldly context).

5) In terms of "this-worldly" and "other-worldly" signifying different spatial locations, e.g., earth and heaven, clearly Christianity but also to a considerable degree Islam are other-worldly while Judaism (in its "official" formulation though, admittedly, not on the popular level) is this-worldly (and indeed even on the popular level where there is a notion of paradise located in heaven, its content consists not only of the spiritual but also of the physical); however, in terms of "this-worldly" and "other-worldly" signifying respectively a physical/materialistic orientation and a non-materialistic/spiritual orientation, Islam is clearly this-worldly (seeing that not only does it stress the physical and the material in the this-worldly existence but that it portrays the existence in its other-world, in its paradise, in very materialistic and physical terms), while Judaism is both this-worldly and other-worldly (seeing that not only does its redemption take place in the spatial location of our world but that the content of the redemption encompasses both the aspect of power and the aspect of personhood, the former being refracted by the latter) and Christianity, again, is quite clearly other-worldly (seeing that not only does the spatial location for the realization of its salvation transcend our world but that the content of its salvation consists in the deliverance of the human from the dimension-of-power thus leaving him being constituted exclusively as a pure person.

6) In Islam every occurrence bar none is predestined by the divine entity and the divine entity rules the world by fiat, precluding the very possibility of questioning or challenging any divine action (or, for that matter, any divine inaction) by excluding any grounding for their ethical evaluation other than the divine commandment (an act is ethically right and good because it is commanded by God and not that God commands it because it is ethically right and good); as against this, in Judaism there is no absolute predestination (while there are different views about the extent of divine control over occurrences, even the most extreme view as that attributed to rabbi Akiva, i.e., "everything is in the hands of heaven except the fear of heaven," leaves some act in human rather than in divine control) and indeed the divine entity is expected always to act justly so that when the testimony of events may suggest that this is not the case, there is no preclusion or, indeed, even the slightest negative evaluation of any questioning or challenge directed towards the divine entity (challenging the divine entity can be encountered throughout the history of Judaism from its inception when Abraham challenges "Is the judge of all the earth not to do justice?" to the present day challenge with respect to the Holocaust); and in Christianity, the divine entity is perceived to relate to the human through grace, i.e., through unmerited, altruistic love, and at the same time, like in Islam but not in Judaism, challenging the divine entity is precluded and predestination, at least in principle, is acceptable, though here, unlike in Islam, the precluded challenging and the accepted feasibility of predestination are associated not with acts of the divine entity in the physical/material this worldly domain but with its acts in extricating the human entity from this domain and transposing it to a purely spiritual otherworldly domain, i.e., in fashioning the human entity as a "new being," an entity that transcends the flesh/body and becomes pure spirit/soul (thus, although Christianity and Islam are at opposite ends of the spectrum between the domain of power and the domain of spirit, or precisely because of this, they, in contradistinction to Judaism, share a common denominator to wit, that in both the divine entity constitutes itself as ultimate essentially in the context of only one dimension and as such its ultimacy is not in any way contracted by its participation in the other dimension).

7) Commensurate with the gradation among the three biblical religions with respect to the way the divine entity relates to the world and, much more significantly, to the human entity, one can note a corresponding gradation with respect to the way the human relates to the divine. Thus, in Islam the human is to be totally submissive to the divine will and completely fatalistic about its own destiny; in Judaism, on the other hand, the human is perceived as a partner to the divine in the work of redemption while in Christianity the human is perceived as the passive recipient/beneficiary of divine grace.

Now we would want to argue that this, albeit short list of comparative observations (a more extensive list that would elaborate on these considerations and indeed add some additional considerations will be submitted below when we have occasion to examine our claim on behalf of each of the three "daughter religions" separately each in its own terms), would support our claims made here (i.e., the claims that Islam formulates itself essentially with reference to power while Christianity formulates itself essentially with reference to spirit, consciousness, and Judaism formulates itself essentially with reference to both power and spirit) because it could be shown that a persuasive rationale and justification could be established for them only on the basis of this claim.

Of course, it can be rightly claimed that by and large not too many, if any, religious formulations that found concrete institutional expression within history, and certainly none of the biblical "daughter religions" with which we are dealing here, are monolithic as regard their content of faith, i.e., that they are constituted by a single strand. Rather, it is true that they are made up of any number of different strands (though it is also true that there is a common denominator underlying the various strands as, for example, Jesus in Christianity, the Halacha in Halachic Judaism, and the sharia in Islam). Still, we would want to argue that with respect to Halachic Judaism and Islam, though admittedly not with respect to Christianity, one can deal with them as if they were monolithic, seeing that the other strands that find expression within them, e.g., the Kabbalah in Halachic Judaism or Sufism in Islam, had to come to terms with the basic orientation of the dominant strands involved in these formulations, i.e., the Halacha in Halachic Judaism and the shari'a in Islam, by submitting, i.e., by yielding, to the basic requirements implicated in their respective orientations, even though such submission necessarily implicated having to compromise their own basic orientation.[2]

At the same time, however, we cannot as already noted make the same claim on behalf of Christianity, for here we fail to encounter a single, specific strand that can be arrogated the status of being the dominant, defining strand and with which all other alternative strands have to come to terms, i.e., avoid a head-on collision, if they are to remain within the same religious phenomenon that is Christianity. Rather, we encounter here, depending on where the origin of Christianity as a separate religious phenomenon distinct from its historical beginnings in the Judaism of the second commonwealth is to be established, two or three self-standing strands which are distinct as far as their respective religious content is concerned (though, of course, they all do share the figure of Jesus as a common denominator). Thus, if we place the origin to be with Paul followed by the Greek and Latin Church fathers, we encounter two major strands, i.e., the Catholic/Orthodox strand and the Protestant strand, while if we place the origin to be with the very appearance of Jesus and his immediate disciples and followers as this is presented in the synoptic gospels, we encounter three strands, i.e., the preceding two strands and a third antecedent strand which we may refer to as the Nazarene strand.[3]

Placing the origin of Christianity as a distinct and separate religious phenomenon in the very appearance of Jesus and his immediate disciples and followers is, however, very problematic. This is so because of two basic considerations. First, the picture presented in the synoptic gospels has no direct, eyewitness historical substantiation. It is a picture presented by people who lived thirty or forty years after the event who had no direct knowledge of Jesus, nor were there any other direct sources available. Thus, we cannot determine whether the picture presented has any historical validity or is but a story, a myth, created *post factum* within an already existing community of faith to account for its origins (in a way, similar to the stories of the patriarchs in the Book of Genesis in the Hebrew Bible). Secondly, even if we accept the historical validity of the narration, a good case can be made that the picture that is presented does not, in the last analysis, betray any substantial break with the fundamental religious orientation of the phenomenon of Judaism in whose midst it arises. In essence it remains within the parameters of the phenomenon of Judaism. Thus, for example, a messianic claim cannot be taken as going against the grain in the phenomenon of Judaism nor can the expectation and hope for the coming kingdom of heaven. We may conclude, therefore, that the Nazarene strand remains with the framework of the phenomenon of Judaism, even more specifically within the pharisaic/rabbinic strand developing within it at that time (after all, there is no abrogation in principle of the Halacha as a whole, only diversion with respect to certain commandments). The distinctiveness of the Nazarene strand lies in its tendency towards an idealistic/altruistic/utopian orientation inclining it in consequence (and indeed in contradistinction to the more mitigated stance characterizing pharisaic/rabbinic Judaism) to the adoption of an other-worldly and an imminent eschatological stance (and this other-worldly stance may well have come about only after and in consequence of the crucifixion in an attempt to counteract the negative connotation that the event implicated with respect to the messianic claim arrogated to Jesus). But, to repeat, this does not constitute a break with the phenomenon of Judaism only the establishment of yet another variant sect among the other sects vying for domination within the Judaism of the first century C.E. In the last analysis, the Nazarene strand remains within the parameters of the phenomenon of Judaism—it is but the strand that among the alternative strands formulates itself most pronouncedly within the context of the dimension-of-consciousness.

The break with the phenomenon of Judaism comes with Paul and as such the valid point of origin for the emergence of the phenomenon of Christianity as a distinct, separate religious formulation must be taken to be with him rather than with the appearance of Jesus and his immediate disciples. For it is Paul (and not Jesus, nor his disciples, nor their successors in the so-called Jerusalem Church) that abrogates the fundamental linkage between the ethnic/national and the religious aspect which for the phenomenon of Judaism (certainly when it formulates itself in terms of its distinctive strand, i.e., the prophetic strand) is an inextricable linkage and it is also he who abrogates the Law as the principal expression of the faith thus cutting out the very heart of the pharisaic/rabbinic strand, the strand that comes to define the phenomenon of Judaism in its Diaspora existence. Now, these fundamental breaks with the phenomenon of Judaism arise in consequence of Paul's basic move to transform the narrative about Jesus into a religious formulation that is to be directed towards the missionizing of the Greco/Roman world. And although it would seem that Paul himself did not adopt to any great extent aspects that ground themselves in the dimension-of-power characterizing pagan Hellenistic religion and indeed, if anything, adopts views that implicate its rejection as, for example, viewing the human predicament to lie in the very presence of the body, the flesh, within the ontological constitution of the human, his transformation of Christianity into a missionizing religion vis-à-vis the Hellenistic world inevitably initiates a process of adopting many elements from the pagan religion, i.e., a religion that formulates itself in the context of the dimension-of-power, characterizing the Roman/Hellenistic world, a process which is greatly expanded and in its essentials brought to completion by the Church Fathers, both the Greek and the Latin Fathers. The final outcome of this process finds its full expression in the religious formulation of the Roman Catholic Church and in that of the Eastern Orthodox Church, the two constituting a single strand as far as the religious content is concerned, i.e., the Catholic/Orthodox strand.

And this being the case, it should not be surprising in the least that in this strand we encounter the religious phenomenon of Christianity in its (at least partial) transformation into a Hellenistic/pagan religious expression as can be witnessed in its adaptation of any number of fundamental aspects that are clearly derivable from within the context of the dimension-of-power. Thus, for example, it can be seen in the notion of the incarnation and in its commensurate notion of sainthood, though the latter notion implicates a reverse direction to that for the former (still, the essential point here is that both notions abrogate the "gap" between the divine entity and the human entity, replacing it with a continuum that links and allows one to become the other, incarnation implicating the divine becoming human and sainthood implicating the human becoming angelic, divine, i.e., *apotheosis*). Secondly, it can be seen in the resort to the sacraments as instruments of sanctification (they being "communal acts" which through their employment of "a specific set of words, gestures and physical elements such as bread, wine, oil and water" communicate the presence and grace of God to the believers) and in particular in the resort to the sacrament of the Eucharist as an instrument of salvation. Thirdly, it can be seen in the adoption of iconography, which is to say in the representation of the divine visually and thus spatially rather than experiencing it auditorily and thus temporally. Fourthly, it can be seen in the division between the sacred and the profane with respect to things, persons and places, the former being accorded sanctity, i.e., heightened power, worship and veneration, while the latter are viewed as mundane, thus introducing a distinction between priesthood and laity and between holy and secular places. These examples and many others, we would submit, can receive their rationale only from within the context of the dimension-of-power, the dimension in which pagan religion, this being the religion of the Greco-Roman world, grounds itself. To the extent, therefore, that the Catholic/Orthodox strand within Christianity adopted itself to the pagan religion of the Hellenistic world, it clearly came to ground itself in the dimension-of-power.

But of course, this does not in principle necessarily implicate that the Catholic/Orthodox strand cannot at the same time also retain to some extent a grounding in the dimension-of-consciousness (and this would in no way affect the validity of our claim here, seeing that the claim refers to a tilting between the two dimensions and not to the cancellation of one dimension in favor of the other). But whether or not the Catholic/Orthodox strand does in fact retain a grounding in the dimension-of-consciousness, and if so to what extent, thus in consequence mitigating its grounding in the dimension-of-power, is a different matter that needs to be ascertained. And here it may seem possible, certainly at first sight, to argue that the Catholic/Orthodox strand does indeed ground itself to some extent in the dimension-of-consciousness. Such argument would in all likelihood base itself, in the main, on two considerations. First, it may be pointed out that notwithstanding its grounding within the pagan religion of the Hellenistic world, the Catholic/Orthodox strand does not completely sever its linkage to the Hebrew bible and consequently to the dimension-of-consciousness as can be ascertained rather persuasively in its structuring of the central form of its worship, i.e., the mass, on the model of the sacrificial cult in the Jerusalem Temple, seeing that the central signification of both forms of worship lies in the belief that atonement can be effected in the sacrificing of a third party (i.e. the animal in the Temple cult and Jesus in the mass) and, closely associated with this, that in ingesting parts of the sacrifice the believer is empowered inasmuch as the sacrifice has been invested with the divine presence. Secondly, and perhaps even more tellingly, it may be pointed out that in incorporating within itself hermetic, mendicant and monastic expressions (expressions embodying themselves in such groups as the deserts hermits, the Cistercians, e.g., the Trappists, the Carmelites, the Benedictines, the Franciscans, and others) the Catholic/Orthodox strand is incorporating expressions that clearly reject the dimension-of-power and ground themselves in the dimension-of-consciousness, seeing that we encounter in these expressions a withdrawal from and indeed a rejection of the concrete material world (see, for example, their resort to a life of poverty and asceticism and indeed to the inflicting of suffering upon the body), thus a rejection of all manifestations of power, turning instead to other-worldly concerns as manifested in a life of prayer and spiritual/mystical contemplation.[4] Thus, the incorporation of these expressions within the Catholic/Orthodox strand would seem to indicate that the grounding within the dimension-of-power which we have arrogated to the Catholic/Orthodox strand may well have to be further qualified and mitigated.

We would submit, however, that some further reflection may well show that the conclusion which we drew from the two foregoing considerations, namely that they lead to a partial grounding of the Catholic/Orthodox strand within the dimension-of-consciousness, may not after all be, in the last analysis, all that valid. For as regards the first consideration (i.e., the consideration that pointed to the close similarity as regards form and signification between the mass in the Catholic/Orthodox strand and the Temple sacrificial cult in the Hebrew bible), the conclusion that the linkage between the Catholic/Orthodox strand and the Hebrew bible can be taken as implicating a grounding of the Catholic/Orthodox strand within the dimension-of-consciousness is rather questionable. This is so, seeing that the linkage to the Hebrew bible here is specifically to its priestly and not to its prophetic strand and that, as already noted above, the priestly strand, although mitigating itself to some extent in order to avoid collision with the prophetic strand, retains in the main its original, indeed its pre-biblical pagan, grounding in the dimension-of-power. As such, the linkage to the Hebrew bible in no way implicates here a grounding within the dimension-of-consciousness. To establish such a grounding would have required a linkage to the prophetic and not the priestly strand and this clearly is not the case here. And as regards the second consideration, while there is no denying that the practices characterizing the hermetic/mendicant/monastic orientation clearly implicate a rejection of this-worldly transactions, thus suggesting a rejection of the dimension-of-power which in turn would imply an embrace of (or, at least, a move towards) the dimension-of-consciousness, if we turn, however, to the goal towards whose realization these practices strive, we seem to be back in the context of the dimension-of-power. For the goal of this orientation in disassociating the human from a this-worldly orientation implicates an ever closer relation of the human to the divine culminating ultimately in their full union, which as such implicates the abrogation of the "gap" between the human and the divine, an abrogation which undermines an essential aspect of the dimension-of-consciousness introducing in its place a continuum between the human and divine, thus re-introducing an aspect that is a fundamental aspect of the dimension-of-power. Thus it is not all that clear that in spite of the many aspects of this orientation that reject the dimension-of-power, the orientation grounds itself in the dimension-of-consciousness. Rather, it would seem that, in the last analysis, the orientation reverts to grounding itself within the dimension-of-power, except that the grounding here assumes a negative rather than a positive signification.

We must conclude, therefore, that the Catholic/Orthodox strand does not really ground itself, in the last analysis, in the dimension-of-consciousness. But even if one were to concede that some mitigation of such a conclusion should be feasible, yielding a state of affairs where the strand grounds itself not only in the dimension-of-power but also, to some extent, in the dimension-of-consciousness (thus falling, to some degree, into the category we arrogated to Halachic Judaism), the tilting between the two dimensions would be predominantly not towards the dimension-of-consciousness but towards the dimension-of-power. And, this being the case, it should be clear that our claim regarding Christianity, namely, that in Christianity we encounter the balance between the two dimensions as being tilted towards the dimension-of-consciousness, cannot be validated if the formulation of Christianity is taken to be defined by the Catholic/Orthodox strand.

To find a validation for the claim that in the phenomenon of Christianity one can encounter a tilting away from the dimension-of-power towards the dimension-of-consciousness we must turn to the other major alternative strand, a strand that broke away from the Catholic/Orthodox strand, for becoming the defining strand for the phenomenon of Christianity, namely, the Protestant strand. And, this being the case, our claim with respect to Christianity is to be taken as being directed primarily to the Christianity that expresses itself in the Protestant strand.[5]

Now, that the Protestant strand tilts the balance between the dimension-of-power and the dimension-of-consciousness towards the dimension-of-consciousness can be ascertained from a negative and from a positive vantage point. From a negative vantage point it can be ascertained in its rejection of aspects adopted in the Catholic/Orthodox strand which ground themselves in the dimension-of-power. Thus, it can be ascertained, for example, in its rejection of the mass, of iconography, of sainthood, of priesthood, of the sacraments, of works as contributing factors in effecting salvation, of penance and dispensation, indeed, in the rejection of specific sets of words, gestures, and physical elements in the format of its worship.[6] Now, in a way such a rejection or, at least, a mitigation of the dimension-of-power would seem indeed to implicate a tilting towards the dimension-of-consciousness, seeing that, as already noted, the dimension-of-consciousness is the only other dimension available, so that the rejection or mitigation of the dimension-of-power per force tilts the balance towards the dimension-of-consciousness. Still, the rejection or mitigation of the dimension-of-power as such would not seem, in the last analysis, to provide a sufficiently persuasive substantiation for our claim. To do that, a substantiation from a positive vantage point is called for. To address this call thus becomes our next task.

Thus, from a more positive vantage point we may cite, for example, the following considerations:

1) The name, or rather the names, arrogated to God here (seeing that in Christianity, as formulated in its doctrine of the trinity, the unitary God manifests Himself not in the form of one persona but in the form of three persona, i.e., as Father, as Son and as Holy Spirit) are basically names that ground themselves, in the last analysis, in the dimension-of-consciousness. This is particularly the case with regard to the manifestation of God in the second persona where the name arrogated to God, i.e., the name of Jesus, is most pronouncedly personal and individualized. Now, it is true that with regard to the names arrogated to God in His first and third persona, i.e., the name of Father and Holy Spirit respectively, we have names that are generic. Still, the signification of these names indicates that they too implicate themselves after all with respect to the dimension-of-consciousness. This can certainly be seen very clearly with respect to the name of the Holy Spirit. But it can also be seen with respect to the name of the Father (even though in the doctrinal formulation its signification is with regard to progeny, i.e., God being the father of Jesus, and as such carrying a biological connotation which as such would place it within the dimension-of-power), seeing that the notion of fatherhood clearly incorporates within itself the connotation of compassion, love, and devotion. In the last analysis, regardless of what view one may take regarding the status of the names arrogated to the first and third persona, the significant and, indeed, decisive factor here is that in His second persona God is arrogated a clear-cut, unambiguous individualized personal name, seeing that it is principally and, indeed, essentially in the manifestation of the second persona that God here is relevant to the religious enterprise

inasmuch as it is in this manifestation that God plays the central (and one might even say the exclusive) role in the drama of salvation and thus is relevant to the human concern.

2) The fundamental attribute arrogated to God is not power (as in Islam) but agape, namely, a one-way, unconditional love.

3) Intimately related to the preceding consideration, salvation is effected solely through grace, namely, through a unilateral salvific act dispensed exclusively by God (though some theological formulations add the further stipulation that for grace to be effective, its acceptance in faith, i.e., in trust, by the human is also required).[7]

4) The notion of resurrection, which necessarily implicates an existence-after-death, clearly locates such existence fully within the realm of the spirit, thus completely separating itself from the material/physical world in which we live here and now. As already noted, this is in stark contrast to the kind of existence-after-death implicated in the notion of resurrection as viewed in Islam where such existence is fully located (and indeed, if anything, is located in a highly exaggerated form) within the material/physical world. (By the way, a further stark contrast, this time vis-à-vis both Christianity and Islam, is presented by Halachic Judaism. Here the existence-after-death is not viewed as offering eternal life in answer to the predicament of the finitude of earthly life but rather as a temporary renewal of life at the end of days to allow the last day of judgment to take place and thus finally attain full and uncompromised justice for all of humanity and so enable us to, so to speak, close the books and set aside the nagging challenge of "the righteous man and he is suffering—the evil man and he is prospering").

5) The focus in the presentation of God here is on His humility, humbleness; He is presented as vulnerable, self-effacing, indeed, as powerless and defenseless. After all, mere humans, i.e. the Roman soldiers, could crucify Him. He is a God who in terms of power is at a complete disadvantage in comparison with human power.[8] Indeed, if the divine entity here were to be grounded within the dimension-of-power, we would have been confronted with an insurmountable contradiction. For the divine entity (which by definition is to be the ultimate entity in whichever dimension it is grounded) when it is grounded within the dimension-of-power must be perceived as possessing power and not just any degree of finite power but infinite power—anything less would be highly problematic. At the same time, however, when it is to be grounded within the dimension-of-consciousness, then not only is the lack of power not a problem but it is actually to be expected and inasmuch as the divine entity here is to be an ultimate entity within the dimension-of-consciousness, its total lack of power is actually dictated—as a pure Thou-being it cannot possess any power whatsoever, His powerlessness is not a deficiency but a virtue. Thus, the presentation of God as being defenseless, vulnerable, humble, powerless necessarily implicates that He is a God who grounds Himself within the dimension-of-consciousness.

6) The implication of Christianity grounding itself in the dimension-of-consciousness rather than in the dimension-of-power can also be encountered in,

so to speak, the other side of the coin of its theological formulation, i.e., of its formulation of God, discussed in the previous consideration, namely, it can be encountered in its anthropological formulation, i.e., in its formulation of the human. This is clearly reflected in the doctrine of original sin which signifies that the human in its present state of falleness cannot help sinning (this state being brought about by Adam's sin of eating from the tree of knowledge of good and evil, it being the original sin both in the sense of being the first instance of sinning but also, and much more significantly, the sin that brings about a fundamental transformation in the ontological constitution of the human). The human given its present ontological constitution is inescapably bound to sin. The specific factor in the ontological constitution of the human that since Paul is seen to be the cause of sinning in the human is the bodily component in the human's constitution—the seat of sin is in the flesh constituting the human. And commensurate to this diagnosis of the human predicament the cure, i.e., the salvation, offered is the transformation of the human into a "new being," a being which would be devoid of flesh, i.e., of the bodily component, thus being constituted exclusively in terms of the spirit. Now, the formulation here of both the predicament and the salvation clearly implicates that it grounds itself within the dimension-of-consciousness, seeing that it negatively evaluates and rejects the flesh, the body, which constitute a clear expression of the dimension-of-power and at the same time positively evaluates and affirms the spirit which constitutes a clear expression of the dimension-of-consciousness.[9]

7) It is important to underline here what has already been noted above, that in the strand of Christianity considered here (i.e., mainly the Protestant strand) God's revelation to the human is mediated through the word and not through a physical/material mediation. For this clearly manifests a grounding within the dimension-of-consciousness, seeing that only within the dimension-of-consciousness (and certainly not within the dimension-of-power) can the word arise inasmuch as only within this context can it carry meaning and thus indeed be a word and not mere sound. Thus, making the word the foundation and, indeed, the centerpiece of the faith clearly implicates a grounding in the dimension-of-consciousness.

8) Just as significant is the fact that the reverse relation to the relation of revelation, namely, the relation of worship (i.e., the relation from the human to God) is equally mediated verbally in an exclusive manner. The format of the worship consists exclusively in the recitation of prayers and the singing of hymns, in other words, it consists of words and music, excluding all physical manifestations such as acts of bowing, kneeling or prostrating. Indeed, the centerpiece of the worship format (even though, strictly speaking, it itself is not an act of worship, i.e., of the human addressing God, but rather an act of the human being addressed by God through the mediation of a fellow human), namely, the act of preaching, the sermon, is exclusively verbal. An additional important further consideration lies in the fact that neither the prayers nor the hymns constituting the format of the worship are in any way fixed or predetermined. No particular prayer or hymn is unalterably attached to any particular worship service.

Rather, they are freely selected from a collection that has been compiled over the years and which has, over the years, undergone changes and will in all likelihood undergo changes in the future. Furthermore, the format of the worship here allows and, indeed, encourages the personal expression of the worshipper in composing his/her own prayers or hymns. The significance of this observation lies in that it precludes the intrusion of magic into the worship format (the essence of magic lying in the fact that the efficacy of the expression or of the act is determined by the precision by which the preset formulation of the expression or of the act are respectively pronounced or carried out). Thus, magic as here defined is clearly an act, be it verbal or physical, which can arise only in the context of the dimension-of-power and consequently its exclusion clearly indicates a grounding within the dimension-of-consciousness.

Now, providing this justification for our claim regarding Christianity as it expresses itself within the Protestant strand (and, for that matter, in the other strands within Christianity which either refrained from entering into or alternatively withdrew in various degrees from a symbiosis with paganism) clearly implicates, in turn, that our claims regarding Islam and Halachic Judaism respectively should be provided with similar justification. Thus regarding our claim with respect to Islam that it tilts the balance towards the dimension-of-power we may cite the following considerations:

1) The sole name arrogated to the divine, i.e., Allah, signifying in Arabic "the divine," is a general and not a personal name. Furthermore, it is a generic name that is completely neutral, namely, that does not include any aspect that may implicate the dimension-of-consciousness. It thus clearly implicates the divine entity as being impersonal. Entities that are personal are individualized and consequently receive individualized names, which evidently is not the case in Islam with respect to the divine entity.[10]

2) The dominant attribute ascribed to the divine entity overshadowing all other attributes, indeed the attribute that captures the very essence of the divine entity (and as such is really the only attribute for all intents and purposes), is power, brute power (the Quran scorns the gods of Paganism on the ground that they are powerless). And, in turn, the very essence of the power attributed to the divine entity is its being infinite. Indeed, any aspect that is deemed to be a possible compromise of that power, such as the Crucifixion, God's resting on the seventh day after creating the world, God being constituted as spirit or the arrogation of the attribute of fatherhood to God (seeing that fatherhood signifies compassion—see the biblical reference to the compassion of the father for his children—and compassion implicates a limitation on the infinity of brute power), is flatly rejected.[11]

3) The power possessed by God is infinite, thus necessarily implicating that every aspect of life and the world is run by Him (otherwise the infinity of God's power would be compromised), in other words, necessarily implicating a totally deterministic view of life and the world and commensurately a completely fatalistic attitude on the part of the human towards them.

4) The positing of God's power as infinite not only implicates total determinism but total predestination with respect to every occurrence in the world and life, which, in turn, implicates arrogating omniscience to God—omnipotence implicates omniscience.

5) The conduct behooving the human in these circumstances is one total of submissiveness (indeed in Arabic, "Islam" means submissiveness); indeed it is a conduct that is seen as being devoid of the capacity of pursuing its own independent action, which is to say that it is a conduct that necessarily implicates its possessor, i.e., the human being, as being completely devoid of free will.[12]

6) The total transcendence of God is greatly emphasized, implicating God's inaccessibility in any direct form. Thus God does not communicate, i.e., reveal Himself, directly, but only through intermediaries, e.g., angels (the Quran is dictated to Muhammad through the angel Gabriel in stark contrast to the direct dictation of the Torah from God to Moses). Indeed, angels play a considerable role in Islamic belief, constituting the second of the four fundamental beliefs of Islam. Similarly, the view of man as being, in any shape or manner, a bearer of the divine image is completely rejected, and so is the aforementioned rejection of the arrogation of the attribute of fatherhood to God—God is never referred to as Father—except that here fatherhood is rejected on the basis of its implicating not compassion as such but rather the close and intimate relation between father and child. The transcendence of God, however, is established not on a qualitative but on a quantitative basis. God is inaccessible not because He is qualitatively "wholly other" but because of the infinity of His power, seeing that any accessibility to Him would compromise His power as regards its infinity.[13]

7) The only appropriate and, indeed, possible disposition on the part of the human is a totally fatalistic disposition, a position which would make sense only within a context in which God is given infinite power and as such is seen as running the world in all its aspects to the smallest detail. This is of course commensurate with the position noted above whereby the only possible attitude vis-à-vis God prescribed to the human is an attitude of total submissiveness. In no conceivable way can man be a partner to God in running the world.

8) The prescription of Jihad in the Quran, or more precisely what is being referred to as the lesser Jihad, again clearly implicates the grounding of Islam within the dimension-of-power, seeing that it places an obligation upon the ruler, i.e., Kalif, in Islam to use force to bring about the conquest of the infidels and consequently their conversion to Islam (the formulation of Jihad, it should be noted, is seen by many Muslims as the sixth constitutive pillar of their faith).[14] The conquered people are to be forcefully converted to Islam by virtue of the fact that Islam has manifested a superiority of power over them. The whole notion of the lesser Jihad, in the very essence of its signification and in the way it is to play itself out, places Islam squarely in the dimension-of-power—Islam is clearly a religion that has committed itself to convert the world of the infidels and this conversion is to be carried out in terms of power.

9) Islam is certainly totally uncompromising in its monotheistic stance. But its monotheism is what might be called arithmetical monotheism (i.e., a mono-

theism that merely signifies the arithmetical oneness of the divine entity) rather than personal monotheism (i.e., a monotheism which while implicating an arithmetical oneness for the divine entity, signifies essentially that the diving entity is a personal being, a Thou being).[15] Now, inasmuch as the overwhelming emphasis in Islam is on the notion of arithmetical monotheism and not on the notion of personal monotheism, i.e., on the arithmetical oneness of the divine entity and not on its personhood, the implication is very clear that the notion of monotheism in Islam precludes its being grounded within the dimension-of-consciousness and instead indicates its being grounded within the dimension-of-power, it being the only available alternative grounding.

10) The attribute arrogated to the divine that is stressed most pronouncedly is that of creator, i.e., God as creator of the world. Now, the attribute of creator of the world is clearly an attribute that can arise only within the context of the dimension-of-power. It is only a God who constitutes Himself in terms of power, i.e., an It-God, that is a God that can be a creator of the world. A God who constitutes Himself in terms of consciousness, i.e., a pure Thou-God, thus a God devoid of power, could not be a creator of the world. Creation is a manifestation of power. Only an entity that possessed power can effect creation.

11) Worship is primarily delineated by *rakatin*, i.e., by the prescribed positions of body and hands. The verbal element in the worship is limited to fixed formulas declaiming praise (mainly with respect to the attribute of power) and obedience to God, each declamation being associated with a particular position of the body and hands. It does not include petitions. This is a form of worship that fits within the dimension-of-power and not within the dimension-of-consciousness, seeing that it is a form of worship whose efficacy is, in the main, contingent on the precise execution of physical acts; it is not worship in the form of address. Such a form of worship is in many ways reminiscent of the way magic or, for that matter, technology operates where the efficacy of the operation is likewise dependent on the precision by which the agent executes pre-set instructions and not on the agent's personal intentions.

12) The notion of life after death is a central and widespread notion in Islam and this points to the notion of finitude as the notion constituting the perceived ultimate predicament and this, seeing that the notion of finitude implicates quantification, clearly implicates, in turn, that the notion of ultimate predicament formulates itself here within the context of the dimension-of-power. This claim is further substantiated, and now no longer from a reflective but from a concrete vantage point, by the additional observation that the notion of life after death is portrayed in Islam in very materialistic, physical terms (the Quran goes into great detail in portraying paradise and hell in very materialistic, physical terms), thus in terms that are fully grounded within the context of the dimension-of-power.

13) Lastly, the thrust of the various observations advanced here is perhaps best summed up in the succinct statement by the Ayatollah Humenei that Islam is politics, thus linking Islam with the notion of the state, seeing that the phenomena of the state and politics constitute themselves on the basis of transac-

tions in power and as such are phenomena that ground themselves within the dimension-of-power.[16]

And, with respect to our claim regarding Halachic Judaism, namely, that it tries to balance its grounding in both the dimension-of-consciousness and the dimension-of-power, we may cite the following considerations:

1) Halachic Judaism following the Hebrew bible arrogates to the divine entity, i.e., to God, two names, namely, the name of Eloha (or, much more commonly, the plural form of Elohim) and the name of Yehova (or in English Yahwe). The former name, being a general, descriptive name, clearly grounds God within the dimension-of-power while the latter name, being a personal, particular, denotative name, grounds God within the dimension-of-consciousness. This is in clear contradistinction to both Islam and Christianity where the naming arrogated to God grounds it, as we have seen, in only one of these two dimensions, either within the dimension-of-power (as is the case in Islam) or within the dimension-of-consciousness (as is the case in Christianity). Thus Halachic Judaism, in holding on to the two names originating within the two main strands in the Hebrew bible, i.e., the priestly and the prophetic, clearly reflects the thrust within Halachic Judaism to keep its grounding within both the dimension-of-consciousness and the dimension-of-power in some kind of balance.

2) Even more telling is the consideration that the essential attribute arrogated to God in Halachic Judaism is that of justice, i.e., of God dealing justly with the human, seeing that the notion of justice signifies by its very essence the attainment of a fair balance between the dimension-of-power and the dimension-of-consciousness, namely, attaining a fair balance between the contradictory implications emanating from the two "stuffs," i.e., power and consciousness, constituting the dimensions respectively, and this necessarily implicates a grounding in both of these two dimensions.[17]

3) This balancing between the dimension-of-consciousness and the dimension-of-power, which the attribute of justice, by its very signification, represents, is further buttressed by an array of further attributes dividing themselves more or less evenly between those grounding themselves in the dimension-of-consciousness and those grounding themselves in the dimension-of-power, thus leading Halachic Judaism to balance itself between the two dimensions. Thus, for example, on the one hand God is referred to as *El Shadai* (God of Power), *Eloha Tz'vaot* (God of the Legions), *El Elyon* (a high God), while on the other hand He is referred to as *El Male Rahamim* (God full of pity), *El Rahum Ve Hanun* (God of pity and compassion), the former references grounding themselves in the dimension-of-power and the latter in the dimension-of-consciousness. This two-fold grounding in both the dimension-of-consciousness and the dimension-of-power is perhaps best summed up in the reference to God as *Avinu Malkenu* (our God, our king) and the petitioning of God in terms of *Ase Imanu Tz'daka VaHesed* (deal with us in righteousness and loving kindness).

4) There is no denying that the tenet of creation and its accompanying tenet of God as creator are fully incorporated into Halachic Judaism. The presentation

in Genesis I of what later in medieval Jewish philosophy was coded *creatio ex nihilo*, i.e., creation out of nothing, was fully adopted by Halachic Judaism.[18] Now, the notion of creation would normally implicate that it is effected through a physical act (which, by the way, is indeed the way it is presented in all the creation myths that arose within the context of pagan religion) and this would clearly further implicate that it is a notion that grounds itself in the dimension-of-power. However, the story of creation as presented in Genesis qualifies itself in two ways which greatly mitigate its grounding in the dimension-of-power. First, creation is effected here not by a physical act but by the spoken word, a verbal act—God creates merely by speaking, by commanding "let there be . . . and it was." Secondly, the story of creation culminates in a state of complete rest, in a complete cessation of all physical activity, thus in a state that is diametrically opposed to that of creation and which as such undermines a grounding in the dimension-of-power.

5) Likewise, there is no denying that providence (i.e., determining and controlling the occurrence and course of events) is arrogated to God in Halachic Judaism and providence is clearly a notion that grounds itself in the dimension-of-power. Unlike Islam and Christianity, however, the providence arrogated to God is not total and all-inclusive. The extent of the providence arrogated may vary as, for example, being limited, on the one hand, to running the course of national destinies (as can be seen in classical biblical prophecy) while, on the other hand, being extended to running the life of the individual human in the minutest detail. But never is the providence arrogated to God total (see the famous statement by Rabbi Akiva "all is in the hands of heaven, except the fear of heaven"). Some space is always left for the human to determine his own life, thus safeguarding his free will, a notion that clearly grounds itself in the dimension-of-consciousness (and which, in turn, endows the human with dignity but also holds him accountable and thus responsible for his actions). In such a context the human is seen not only as bearing the image of the divine but as being a partner to God in running the world.[19]

6) The notion of resurrection, like the notion of creation, does not originate within the religious phenomenon of Judaism but enters it from external sources (most notably from Persian Zoroastrian sources), except that unlike the notion of creation, which enters the phenomenon in its biblical expression at its earliest stages, the notion of resurrection enters the phenomenon, for all intents and purposes, post-biblically in its Halachic expression (there may be some passing reference to the notion in the very late biblical sources manifesting apocalyptic orientation like the book of Daniel).[20] Now, in contradistinction to Islam, on the one hand, where the notion of the afterlife that is linked to the notion of the resurrection is depicted in very materialistic/physical terms and where therefore the grounding of the notion of resurrection in the dimension-of-power is not mitigated and, on the other hand, in contradistinction to Christianity where the notion of the afterlife that is linked to the notion of the resurrection is depicted, in stark opposition to Islam, in very spiritual, i.e., contra materialistic/physical, terms (implicating the transformation of the human into a "new being" devoid of

flesh and body) and where therefore the grounding of the notion of resurrection in the dimension-of-power is greatly mitigated, in Halachic Judaism we encounter an in-between position where by virtue of the notion of resurrection being linked primarily not to the notion of the afterlife but rather to the notion of justice (in other words, where the perceived predicament is not the finitude of human existence but the problematic of theodicy), the grounding in the dimension-of-power implicated by the notion of the afterlife is not totally abrogated but rather considerably mitigated towards the dimension-of-consciousness (like the very notion of justice itself it situates itself between the dimension-of-power and the dimension-of-consciousness).[21]

7) The category of worship in Halachic Judaism (i.e., the category comprising the communication from the human to the divine) situates itself also at a midpoint between grounding itself in the dimension-of-power and grounding itself in the dimension-of-consciousness. Thus, on the one hand, its grounding in the dimension-of-power is reflected in the fact that its structure is completely predetermined and does not allow flexibility or spontaneity. Also, it is reflected in that it requires that it be performed as prescribed with precision. These traits may well suggest a resemblance to the traits characterizing the practice of magic, a practice that can receive its rationale only within the context of the dimension-of-power. Indeed, that we encounter these traits in the structure of worship instituted within Halachic Judaism, i.e., traits that implicate a grounding in the dimension-of-power, should not be surprising, seeing that the structure of worship instituted in Halachic Judaism is modeled after the structure of worship instituted in the Jerusalem Temple in conjunction with the sacrificial cult and that this structure of worship is clearly a structure that grounds itself in the dimension-of-power. (Indeed, the structure of worship in Halachic Judaism is instated only as a temporary substitute for the sacrificial cult for the duration in which the Jerusalem Temple remains unavailable, seeing that after the Josianic reform of 621 B.C.E. the performance of the sacrificial cult was restricted to the Jerusalem Temple). On the other hand, however, inasmuch as the physical acts implicated in the performance of the sacrificial cult are replaced by verbal expressions, i.e., by prayers, in the structure-of-faith which Halachic Judaism develops as a substitute for the sacrificial cult, a grounding of the structure-of-faith in the dimension-of-consciousness is clearly added to the grounding in the dimension-of-power which Halachic Judaism inherits from the priestly strand in the Hebrew bible. Thus, given these two aspects which come to characterize the structure of worship in Halachic Judaism, namely, the aspect of being predetermined and preset and the aspect of being constituted by verbal expressions, Halachic Judaism is clearly balancing a grounding in the dimension-of-power with a grounding in the dimension-of-consciousness.

This then is a sample of considerations that can be advanced, it would seem to us, in support of our claim that within the more general observation that all three biblical "daughter religions" ground themselves in both the dimension-of-power and the dimension-of-consciousness, Islam tends to tilt the balance towards the dimension-of-power while Christianity tends to tilt the balance towards the dimension-of-consciousness and Halachic Judaism tends toward balancing the two dimensions.[22]

Now, given the claims put forth here, the further question inevitably arises as to whether this division among the three "daughter religions" regarding their respective groundings is arbitrary or whether there is some rationale for it. Namely, how is one to understand the division among the three "daughter religions" with regard to their respective grounding within the two dimensions. One possibility is to suggest that their respective grounding is arbitrary. Given the fact that we are dealing here within a context that is being constituted by two dimensions, the dimension-of-power and the dimension-of-consciousness, and that this, in turn, implicates three theoretical possibilities of grounding, i.e., a grounding tilting towards the dimension-of-power, a grounding tilting towards the dimension-of-consciousness and a grounding seeking to balance itself between the two dimensions, it is certainly possible that these possibilities would actually find expression within the realm of concrete history. True, there is no inherent necessity that this should have taken place, or that all three possibilities rather than two or one should have found expression within concrete history or that, indeed, they would have found expression in the format that concrete history presents to us, namely, that the theoretical possibility of tilting towards the dimension-of-power would have found expression in Islam, the theoretical possibility of tilting towards the dimension-of-consciousness would have found expression in Christianity and the possibility of retaining a balance between the two dimensions would have found expression in Halachic Judaism. That this is nonetheless what we encounter in concrete history is therefore purely arbitrary. It must be attributed to mere chance, to mere coincidence. It could have been otherwise.

The foregoing scenario is certainly feasible. Still, it would seem to us that an alternative scenario, a scenario that would allow us to push beyond arbitrariness and provide us with a rationale for the particular way in which the three daughter religions accommodate their respective grounding, is feasible. In this scenario a rationale for why Islam, but not the other religions, tilts its grounding towards the dimension-of-power, why Christianity, but not the other religions, tilts its grounding towards the dimension-of-consciousness and why Halachic Judaism, but not the other religions, strives to keep a balance between the two dimensions would be provided by the circumstances which respectively characterize the establishment and "success" of these religions. Thus, Islam tilts its grounding toward the dimension-of-power because the milieus in which it originated, i.e., the Arabian peninsula, and in which it spread through conquest and active missionizing, i.e., Africa and parts of Asia, have been milieus deeply steeped in unintellectualized paganism, having a very low standard of living and requiring a strenuous struggle to maintain oneself in existence. In such circumstances the need for and appreciation of power would be very pronounced and bring about, in turn, a sympathetic acceptance of any religion that formulates itself in a noticeable way within the dimension-of-power.

Christianity, on the other hand, tilts towards the dimension-of-consciousness because the milieus in which it originated, i.e., the Jewish second commonwealth at the beginning of the first century B.C.E.,[23] and to which it spreads through missionizing, i.e., the large slave population in the Roman empire, on the one hand, and members of the Roman establishment, on the other hand (in this latter case, however, power is negated not by its absence but by its failure to ultimately provide full meaning to life) are milieus which, in the last analysis, are devoid of power (in this respect the milieus here are similar to the milieus in which Islam arose, except that in the milieus where Islam arose the possibility of gaining power was, at least in principle, available while in the milieus where Christianity arose the possibility of gaining power was very remote, or, as in the case of the Roman establishment, beside the point). In these circumstances, the religious formulation that would be appealing is not one that offers increased access to power (this would be unrealistic or meaningless) but one that offers an alternative, which by substituting itself in the place of power as the source of life's meaningfulness would overcome the predicament of the lack or the meaninglessness of power. And this is precisely what Christianity, in tilting its grounding towards the dimension-of-consciousness, is in a position to offer. By replacing power with spirit, imperialistic self-centeredness with saintly renunciation, a realistic this-worldliness with an idealistic, utopian other-worldliness, Christianity offers a way of overcoming the lack or meaninglessness of power by negating the significance of power. Instead of glorifying the possession of power it preaches meekness and submissiveness. Not power but weakness will, in the last analysis, embrace salvation. Clearly, such preaching would be very appealing to people who are devoid of power with no realistic possibility of gaining it or to people who find that the possession of power, no matter how extensive it may be, fails to provide their lives with meaningfulness. To such people the claim "Christianity is suffering" would be very meaningful.

Lastly, as regards the circumstances that characterize the establishment and "success" of Halachic Judaism, they too, like the circumstances that characterize the establishment and "success" of Islam and Christianity, involve the deprivation of power. But unlike the case of Islam and Christianity where the deprivation of power precipitates a predicament that is in terms of the lack of power as such, in the case of Halachic Judaism the predicament precipitated by the deprivation of power is not in terms of the lack of power as such but rather in terms of a predicament that is closely linked to and, indeed, implicated by the predicament of the deprivation of power, to wit, by the predicament of the loss of sovereignty. And the predicament of the loss of sovereignty may (though not necessarily) further implicate the predicament of exile-existence, which in turn may (though again not necessarily) further implicate diaspora-existence (exile-existence signifying existence outside one's homeland in someone else's homeland while diaspora-existence signifying existence outside one's homeland that is scattered among different other peoples' homelands). In the case of the Jewish people the predicament of loss of sovereignty did indeed express itself in the further predicament of exile-existence in the form of diaspora-existence. Now, the exile-existence which came to characterize the existence of the Jewish people could well have signified the demise of the religion of Judaism had that religion been a run-of-the-mill religion belonging to the same category of religion to which all the other religions up to that time belonged, namely, belonging to the category of pagan religion. For all pagan religions are in their very essence nature religions, i.e., religions which constitute themselves within the context of nature,[24] and as such they are religions that situate themselves in the context of space as indeed can be clearly seen in the fact that the encounter with the divine entity within these religions is confined to specific locations in space to the exclusion of all other spatial locations (and such locations, by the way, being consequently distinguished as being sacred in contradistinction from all the other locations in space which remain profane). And this, in turn, means of course that pagan religions cannot survive in the circumstances associated with exile-existence, seeing that in these circumstances they are disconnected from their respective sacred locations and that consequently the feasibility of their having contact with their respective divine entities is abrogated. Indeed, being placed in exile-existence, i.e., being placed in a location outside their original location, signified for pagan religions their demise.

The religious formulation that arises within Halachic Judaism, however, presents us with an exception. For here we encounter a religious formulation that can and indeed did survive within exile-existence. The factor that makes this possible is the fact that Halachic Judaism in grounding itself, albeit partially, within the biblical prophetic strand adopts in a significant sense and to a considerable extent the religious formulation that arises within the prophetic strand. This is so inasmuch as in the prophetic strand we encounter a religious formulation which, in contrast to the religious formulation encountered in paganism, does not constitute itself in the context of nature and thus of space but rather in the context of history and thus of time—the divine entity is encountered here not in particular locations in nature but in particular events in history. As such, exile-existence, i.e., existence that implicates the removal of the religion from its sacred places, does not have to implicate the abrogation of the feasibility of encountering the divine entity, thus implicating, in turn, the demise of the religion. Encountering the divine entity in the events of history rather than in locations of space allows the religion that arises within the prophetic strand to function and thus survive in exile-existence. Thus, to the extent that Halachic Judaism grounds itself in the prophetic strand, it adopts this kind of religion, i.e., a religion for which exile-existence would not necessarily implicate its demise.

Still, while this may well account for the feasibility of the survival of the religious phenomenon in exile-existence when it is situated within the context of Halachic Judaism, it does not account for the feasibility of the survival of the nation, i.e., of the Jewish people, in exile-existence when it situates itself within the context of Halachic Judaism. To account for this we must turn to another aspect of the religion that arises within the prophetic strand and which Halachic Judaism adopts when it grounds itself in the prophetic strand. Namely, the religion arising within the prophetic strand is a religion for which the fundamental predicament is the absence of a fully realized righteous society and, commensurate to this, its main vocation is the striving to attain the establishment of such a society. But such a notion of the fundamental predicament and commensurate to it of the religious vocation necessarily requires and thus implicates the presence and availability of a national collectivity. One cannot pass a judgment that a righteous society is absent or urge the striving towards the attainment of such a society if a national collectivity is not available. To have both this kind of basic predicament and this kind of religious vocation feasible, the presence of a national collectivity is a condition *sine qua non* (all alternative kinds of collectivities such as, for example, the family, professional or political associations, communities of faith fall short of encompassing all the relevant aspects that the notion of righteousness should encompass as, for example, the economic, the political, the social or the legal aspects).

And indeed within the prophetic strand the religious phenomenon is inextricably bound to the category of nationhood—the nation is constituted by the religion (indeed, according to the biblical narration in Exodus, the nation is constituted at the encounter at Sinai in conjunction with the constituting of the religion of Judaism, and until that encounter takes place the boundary of the nation is left vague and imprecise, seeing that it comprises itself as an *erev rav*, i.e., a mixed multitude). Unlike all other nations it is not constituted by a genetic common denominator or even by the common denominator of ethos. Indeed, the Jewish nation can be and indeed is, genetically speaking, quite a mixture, an *erev rav*. And due to its dispersion among various host nations possessing different ethos, implicated in its diaspora-existence, different segments of the Jewish nation inevitably came to be influenced by different ethos and consequently came to adopt and incorporate different features into their own ethos (see, for example, the differences in ethos manifesting themselves in the Sephardic and Ashkenazic segments of the Jewish community, most poignantly perhaps in having two different everyday spoken languages, namely, Ladino, which connects with Spanish, and Iddish, which connects with German). Yet, this in no way undermined the unity of the Jewish nationhood. For what has kept the Jewish collectivity together and thus safeguarding Jewish nationhood was, in the last analysis, the religion of Judaism, in particular, the religion of Judaism in its halachic, i.e., legal, expression (even more precisely, in the main the ritualistic, the family and to some extent the commercial parts of the law, seeing that in exile-existence it is these parts, and not the criminal or political parts, that could and were operative). As such, therefore, the feasibility of the survival of the religion of Judaism necessarily meant also the feasibility of the survival of Jewish nationhood.[25]

But while this is certainly the upside of the adoption by Halachic Judaism of the religious formulation of the biblical prophetic strand, there is also a serious downside to that adoption. For inasmuch as the vocation of the religion formulating itself within the context of the biblical prophetic strand is to attain the establishment of a righteous society, the feasibility of striving to attain that goal is clearly made contingent on the availability of sovereignty. In the absence of sovereignty this vocation is no longer feasible and a religious formulation that is devoid of a vocation becomes vacuous, i.e., emptied of its content, and as such is, for all intents and purposes, dead. Thus, if the religious formulation of Halachic Judaism were exclusively the religious formulation adopted from the biblical prophetic strand, it could not have survived in exile-existence even though it could overcome the problematic of being separated from its own land, seeing that it could not have sovereignty at its disposal and consequently it would have been devoid of its religious vocation which, in turn, would have meant that notwithstanding its ability to survive in exile-existence it would have been devoid of its *raison d'être*. Halachic Judaism overcomes this impasse by deriving its religious formulation not only from the biblical prophetic strand but also conjointly from the biblical priestly strand, deriving from the latter its ritualistic codes of law which can now serve as a content for its religious vocation and thus making it viable and operative in the context of its exile-existence.[26] Halachic Judaism could successfully adapt to exile-existence because it grounded itself in both the prophetic and the priestly strands of the biblical tradition, namely, in both the dimension-of-consciousness and the dimension-of-power. It took a grounding in both dimensions for Halachic Judaism to successfully adapt itself to exile-existence—a grounding in one or the other dimension would not have sufficed in itself.

These then are the circumstances that effect the origination and shape the expression of the three biblical "daughter religions," namely, Halachic Judaism, Christianity and Islam.

Notes

1. We resort to the appellation of Halachic Judaism to refer to the religious phenomenon of Judaism as it expressed itself from the close of the biblical period (and a period of transition expressing itself in the period of the second commonwealth) symbolized in the destruction of the first temple in 70 C.E., to the onset of the era of Jewish Emancipation in the 18th century C.E. symbolized by the French Revolution in 1789 C.E. This appellation seems to us to be the most appropriate one, seeing that the religious phenomenon of Judaism during this period grounds itself in the legal corpora contained in the Pentateuch as it is explicated, and indeed by way of that explication considerably expanded, by the Talmudic rabbis (and to a much lesser degree by subsequent rabbinic commentaries through the ages). As such the Law, i.e., the Halacha, comes to define the religious phenomenon of Judaism during this period (and being the only factor that defines the phenomenon during this period, it constitutes the phenomenon, for all intents and purposes, as monolithic).

It bears stressing, however, that this appellation of Halachic Judaism applies to the religious phenomenon of Judaism only with respect to the period designated here, namely, from the latter part of the 1st century C.E. to the 18th century C.E. It cannot be applied to the religious phenomenon of Judaism in the era of Jewish Emancipation. For in this era, for any number of reasons that we shall have occasion to address below, the fundamental grounding of the religious phenomenon of Judaism in the Law (thus having the grounding in the Halacha define the phenomenon) breaks down thus giving rise to any number of alternative formulations that reject the ultimate authority of the Halacha (see, for example, the position held by the Reform movement and the Reconstructionist movement). And while the halachic formulation continues to find expression within the religious phenomenon of Judaism, it is no longer the sole or, indeed, the defining formulation. The halachic formulation can no longer be identified with the religious phenomenon of Judaism as a whole but only with one movement within the phenomenon, i.e., the Orthodox movement. Indeed, as such the modern era up to this point in time should be viewed as a period of transition in the same way that the period from the latter part of the 2nd century B.C.E. to the latter part of the 1st century C.E. is to be viewed as a period of transition to the era of Halachic Judaism.

Lastly, it should be noted that not infrequently two different appellations are being applied to the religious phenomenon of Judaism during the period designated here, to wit, the appellation of Rabbinic Judaism and that of Talmudic Judaism. But as already noted, our preference is for the appellation of Halachic Judaism and this for two reasons. First, the appellations of Rabbinic Judaism and Talmudic Judaism refer in their signification either to the religious leaders implicated in the religious phenomenon of Judaism under discussion here (as is the case in the appellation of Rabbinic Judaism) or to the text constituting its foundation (as is the case in the appellation of Talmudic Judaism), and as such are, in our judgment, at a significant disadvantage in comparison to the appellation of Halachic Judaism, seeing that it refers to the very essence of the theological formulation characterizing the phenomenon, while the alternative appellations impinge upon institutional or textual aspects characterizing the phenomenon. Secondly, the appellation of Rabbinic Judaism (but also that of Talmudic Judaism) is not infrequently applied exclusively to the period from the second to the sixth century C.E., the period in which the Talmud was redacted. Since we are dealing with the phenomenon as it expresses itself in a much longer period and varied circumstances from the period in which the Talmud was redacted, using the appellation of Rabbinic or Talmudic Judaism may be confusing. In view of these considerations we shall use here the appellation of Halachic Judaism.

2. Thus, for example, this can be seen very clearly in Halachic Judaism with respect to the Kabbalistic strand. The Kabbalah had to mitigate the pantheistic orientation implicated in its basically mystical formulation to a panentheistic orientation (proposing, so to speak, to eat the cake and have it too) in order to avoid a head-on collision and come to a *modus vivendi* with Halachic Judaism, whose basic formulation implicated the theistic orientation. Put more specifically and indeed more tellingly, the Kabbalah had to mitigate the ultimate stage of *unio mystica* as the stage of the total absorption of the human within the divine to the notion of *D'vekut*. Similarly in Islam (although the picture here may be less clear-cut, seeing that though the official position of Islam is thoroughly theistic, pantheistic tendencies cannot be excluded), a good case can be made that, in the last analysis, the mystical strand of Sufism is being contained within Islam only because it avoids a head-on collision with the Shari'a.

3. Our incorporation of both the Roman Catholic formulation and the Eastern Orthodox formulation in one single strand rather than in two separate strands is grounded in our contention that their diversion expresses itself in the main on the institutional level and not on the level of the religious content (as such, their diversion is similar to that encountered between the Shi'a and Sunni formulations within Islam which, by the way, is likewise the consideration leading us not to treat them as two distinct strands within Islam). Inasmuch as our concern here focuses on the aspect of the religious content and, even more significantly, that our analysis of it is directed by the criterion which is defined by the bifurcation between the dimension-of-power and the dimension-of-consciousness, we feel justified in incorporating both the Roman Catholic and the Eastern Orthodox formulation in the same strand (as we indeed did with regard to the Sunni and Shi'a formulations within Islam). For we would submit that a persuasive case can be made that in

the last analysis both the Roman Catholic and the Eastern Orthodox formulation manifested in the context of formulating their religious content the similar tendency of adopting a variety of aspects which express the orientation of the dimension-of-power.

And as to the strand referred to by us as the Nazarene strand, it is, to state it very briefly, the strand that constitutes itself in terms of the picture put forth in the synoptic gospels of an allegedly historic person, a Jew named Jesus living in Palestine in the early part of the first century C.E., the religious content of the picture basing itself on the preaching and deeds of that person, i.e., on his words and acts.

4. Clearly, these expressions have a closer kinship to the religious orientation expressed in the synoptic gospels (the orientation that we referred to as that of the Nazarene strand) and also, as we shall presently want to argue, to the orientation of the Protestant strand, except that they occupy the extreme pole with respect to the aspect of the withdrawal from the concrete material world while the Nazarene strand occupies a stance that expresses a more mitigated withdrawal and the Protestant stand occupies a middle position. Of course the Protestant strand has any number of sub-strands, and they differ considerably in the stance they take with respect to this all-important aspect. Thus, for example, the various charismatic Pentecostal sects are most extreme in turning their religious orientation away from the concrete material world towards the spiritual realm, thus from the dimension-of-power to the dimension-of-consciousness. On the other hand, Lutheranism basically views this concrete material world as merely a transitional stage and thus is, in the main, neutral to its concerns, i.e., not being particularly involved in its affairs, with the exception of securing order and stability. And lastly, to cite one more important sub-strand, Calvinism is quite involved in the concrete material world, directing its concern to fashioning a communal life in accordance with its religious orientation. Still, not only in these but also in all the other sub-strands constituting the strand of Protestantism here there is a clear tilting towards the dimension-of-consciousness. The difference is only in the degree of the tilting.

5. True, our claim that the Protestant strand is tilting towards the dimension-of-consciousness implicates a linkage between it and the expression of Christianity that is reflected in the picture presented in the synoptic gospels, i.e., in what can be referred to as the Nazarene strand or primitive Christianity, seeing that the latter also grounds itself in the main within the dimension-of-consciousness. Indeed the Protestant strand itself seems to implicate this linkage in its adoption of the slogan "back to scripture" as its watchword and the slogan "sola scriptura" as its primary guiding principle for formulating its content of faith. Likewise, our claim also implicates a further linkage between the Protestant strand and the monastic orientation (even though the Protestant strand rejects the institution of monasticism), seeing that the monastic orientation also seems to ground itself in the dimension-of-consciousness. (By the way, with respect to their being in a this-worldly orientation, the Protestant strand situates itself between the Nazarene strand and the monastic expression. The Nazarene in being eschatological in its orientation remains to some extent involved in a this-worldly orientation while the monastic expression in withdrawing from this world abrogates any this-worldly concern, though, of course, commensurate to there being different degrees of withdrawal in its various manifestations there will be different degrees of abrogation of the this-worldly concern; as against both, the Protestant strand in submitting to its existence within this world but remaining uninvolved with its potentialities for growth and perfection, merely tolerating it as the place for the human to mark time while awaiting his/her ultimate release from this world, situates itself in-between the two preceding alternatives.) But while a grounding in the dimension-of-consciousness can be encountered in the alternative two instances cited here (and indeed possibly in other instances within the phenomenon of Christianity), it is the

Protestant strand that can provide the most persuasive support to our claim (after all, the Nazarene strand remains within the confines of the phenomenon of Judaism preceding the emergence of Christianity as a distinct, separate, religious phenomenon and monasticism does not constitute itself as a strand but merely as an expression).

Lastly, we may observe that a further implication of the examination pursued here is that when viewed from the vantage point of the religious content, one really has, in the last analysis, with respect to the phenomenon of Christianity two and not three possible alternative strands, the Nazarene and the Protestant strands being joined in one strand, the strand that tilts its grounding towards the dimension-of-consciousness. The possibility of having three possible strands, which was entertained above, arises only when the phenomenon of Christianity is viewed from the chronological vantage point. When it is viewed from the vantage point of the religious content we can only have two possible strands, the Catholic/Orthodox strand and the Protestant/Nazarene strand.

6. Of course, like any concrete historical expression within the religious phenomenon, the Protestant strand is not monolithic in its expression. Indeed, there are varying gradations in how far the tilting from the dimension-of-power towards the dimension-of-consciousness is pursued within the Protestant strand. Perhaps, the least radical shift can be encountered in Luther who, for example, retains after all two of the sacraments and while not retaining the formulation of transubstantiation maintained within the Catholic/Orthodox strand, does not go as far as subsequent formulations within the Protestant strand to adopt a symbolic commemorative formulation but turns to the formulation of consubstantiation as a replacement. A more radical shift can be encountered in Zwingli and Calvin (though the emphasis in Calvin on the absolute domination of God and in consequence of this the adoption of predestination, indeed double predestination, the encouragement of the believer to pursue earthly affairs and the involvement of the faith in the political affairs of the community would seem to implicate a retreat towards the dimension-of-power; indeed, some have claimed a similarity between Calvinism and Islam). And the shift becomes even more radical as one moves progressively beyond these "classical" formulations to the formulations of the Baptists, Anabaptists, Seventh Day Adventists, Evangelicals, Pentecostals and finally, if they are still to be retained within the pale of Christianity, the Unitarians (and commensurately within Christian academic theology to the Ritschlian theologians who move away from focusing on the divinity of Jesus to seeing him as the man of perfect faith and morality thus serving as a paradigm to the rest of humankind). Needless to say, the further down one moves within this progression of formulations that arise within the Protestant strand, the stronger the substantiation for our claim that Christianity as it expresses itself within the Protestant strand manifests a tilt towards the dimension-of-consciousness becomes.

7. We seem to have here a similarity with Islam in that in both formulations God is the sole active agent with the human being merely a passive recipient (and this being, by the way, in clear contrast to the view taken in Judaism where the human is seen as a full partner of God in the work of redemption). Within this similarity, however, where the activity is relegated exclusively to God, Islam and Christianity are at opposite poles in the way they perceive the nature of the activity and God's role in it. In Islam it is predominantly within the realm of power. God is the sole agent in dispensing pleasure and/or suffering to the human, which is to say, of increasing and/or decreasing the level of power possessed by the human (the former manifesting God's reward while the latter manifests His punishment). In Christianity, on the other hand, the activity is predominantly within the realm of the spirit where power is transcended and thus indeed negated. God delivers the human from the constraints of Power (i.e., the flesh) that define him in his fallen state and transforms the human into a "new being," a second Adam, constitut-

ing him purely within the realm of the spirit. Indeed, the other similarities that may be observed between Islam and Christianity as, for example, the similarity between Islam and the Calvinist formulation within Christianity with respect to the doctrine of predestination or, for that matter, the similarity with respect to the notion of resurrection (which, by the way, is the next consideration to be cited here) reveal the same fundamental opposition between Islam and Christianity.

8. By the way, a case can perhaps be made that the occurrence of the Crucifixion played a significant role in making the messianic claim unacceptable to the majority of the Jewish community who could not fathom a crucified Messiah. Indeed, the Crucifixion may well have presented an equally serious problematic to the early Christian community and that the doctrine of the second coming was advanced in order to overcome or, at least, mitigate this problematic.

9. The doctrine of original sin clearly implicates the negation of free will, namely, the capability of the human to choose, and this may certainly precipitate a serious problematic for many theologians, seeing that it necessarily cancels out the possibility of viewing the human as accountable and thus responsible for his actions, and this in turn clearly abrogates the possibility of viewing the human as person.

In response to this, one can encounter a number of various attempts to overcome, or at least mitigate, the problematic. Perhaps the most notable attempt in recent Christian theology is the attempt by Reinhold Niebuhr. Niebuhr understands sin in terms of pride—pride is the manifestation of sin—and he understands pride in terms of human finitude, namely, pride is the manifestation of the human failing to accept his finitude and live by the constraints it imposes, believing himself to be the ultimate sovereign of his life and thus possessing unrestricted power to attain whatever he desires. Given this context, pride, i.e., sin, is, according to Niebuhr, inevitable but not necessary. And being only inevitable but not necessary, it does not abrogate free will with respect to the human. The distinction between "inevitable" and "necessary," which is introduced here, does not seem to us, however, to have, so to speak, any "cash value," seeing that the two terms seem to signify the same state of affairs. For after all, if something is inevitable it is also inescapably necessary and if it is necessary it would, of course, be inevitable. Thus, to say that something is inevitable but not necessary would seem to us to be a contradiction in terms and as such therefore it cannot overcome the problematic precipitated by the doctrine of original sin with respect to the issue of free will. The problematic here would be overcome if we substitute "in all likelihood" for "inevitable." There would be no contradiction to say that the human would in all probability sin but that his sinning is not necessary, and taking this position would clearly not precipitate any problematic with regard to the issue of free will (this, by the way, is a position that would seem to be acceptable within the context of Judaism and which, indeed, is in conformity with the fact that Judaism, both in its biblical and in its halachic expression, does not adopt the formulation of original sin). But of course such an interpretation of what is to constitute the signification of the notion of inevitability would necessarily implicate the cancellation of the doctrine of original sin, seeing that the very thrust of the doctrine is to claim the inescapability and not merely the all likelihood of sinning. Thus, this interpretation of Niebuhr's proposed distinction between the inevitable and the necessary would not do given that Niebuhr wants to retain the doctrine of original sin (we should note here that Niebuhr's formulation here is in most respects very close to the position that can be encountered within the prophetic strand within the Hebrew bible and in Halachic Judaism—indeed, Niebuhr is the most "Jewish" of all Christian theologians. Still, he clearly remains a Christian theologian and this clearly reflects itself in his retention of the doctrine of original sin).

It is possible, however, to advance an alternative interpretation to the distinction between "inevitable" and "necessary" introduced by Niebuhr. According to this interpretation, the distinction lies not with respect to their respective significations (as was the case in the former interpretation) but rather with respect to their respective references. Namely, while it would be readily granted that both "inevitable" and "necessary" bear the same signification, "inevitable" would be designated to refer to the disposition within the human towards sinning while "necessary" would be designated to refer to the human actually perpetrating acts of sinning. Thus, one could maintain without contradiction that while the human is inevitably (i.e. necessarily) disposed towards sinning, his/her actually committing acts of sinning is not necessary (i.e. inevitable). There is no contradiction in saying that the human is inevitably disposed to sin but that he/she does not necessarily have to sin. As such, Niebuhr can, so to speak, eat his cake and have it too, namely, hold on to the doctrine of original sin and at the same time maintain the feasibility of the notion of free will—original sin as formulated here does not undermine human free will.

This interpretation seems to fit nicely into Niebuhr's position, lending it the needed rational underpinning for its formulation. But although, as we have noted, it allows Niebuhr to hold on to the doctrine of original sin and thus retain some linkage with the orientation of Christianity, it nonetheless, given our interpretation of it, cannot really reverse the serious veering away from the orientation of Christianity which Niebuhr's position clearly implicates. After all, the fact remains that in terms of this formulation, the human, in the last analysis, does not have to actually sin. And this is really much more the position of Judaism than of Christianity. Niebuhr thus adds a further consideration that shifts his position back towards the orientation of Christianity. This added consideration links itself to the claim that, given the finitude of the human, the human by his/her own power could not overcome the possibility of his/her disposition to sin realizing itself in an actual act of sinning. Although in principle the human's disposition to sin need not realize itself in actual sinning, the human in his/her own power cannot actually bring it about. In the last analysis, this can be done only by God through an act of grace. Such a view clearly reflects a Christian rather than a Jewish orientation, seeing that it shifts the focus from the human as a partner to God in the work of redemption to the sole role that God plays in the drama of salvation (we use "redemption" for the overcoming of the predicament when it is carried out in a this-worldly context and "salvation" when it is carried out in an other-worldly context).

In this connection it is significant to note that the predicament which is, so the speak, the negative factor in the formulation (i.e., the factor that is to be overcome, to be cancelled out) is viewed as being grounded within the dimension-of-power, seeing that the predicament constitutes itself in terms of the finitude (finitude being the source providing the occasion for pride, the act of sin par excellence, to arise, thus reflecting the fallen state of the human) and that finitude is a notion that clearly implicates quantification, an unmistaken expression of the dimension-of-power. At the same time the salvation which is the positive factor in the formulation (i.e., the factor that overcomes the predicament) is viewed as being grounded within the dimension-of-consciousness, seeing that it constitutes itself in terms of grace (i.e., the sin of pride being overcome by the infusion of grace into the human), and that grace is an unmistaken expression of the dimension-of-consciousness. Thus, Niebuhr's position here reflects the orientation of Christianity which anticipates the transformation of the human from the dimension-of-power to the dimension-of-consciousness and as such lends support to our claim that Christianity tilts the balance between the dimension-of-power and the dimension-of-consciousness towards the dimension-of-consciousness.

10. Indeed, when we wish to personalize an inanimate entity as, for example, a boat or an airplane, we give it an individualized personal name. Also, our stating that Allah is the sole name arrogated to the divine entity is not contradicted by the fact that there are 99 additional names (the 99 beautiful names) ascribed to the divine entity in the Quran and in the tradition (for example, in Al Ghazalli). For these are really names of attributes ascribed to the divine entity, albeit attributes that signify the essence of the divine entity. In any case, these names too clearly point to the dimension-of-power, seeing that they are divided almost equally between names signifying the power and majesty of the divine entity and the names signifying its beauty and infinite attractiveness (this latter signification being also derived from within the context of the dimension-of-power though in a less direct fashion than that of the former signification—beauty and indeed also knowledge are attributes whose signification arises from within the context of the dimension-of-power).

11. True, justice is also ascribed to God, but in the last analysis, it is a vacuous attribution, seeing that all of God's acts are apriori predetermined as being just. Justice does not possess an independent status so that it can serve as a criterion by which God's acts can be evaluated and judged. God's acts cannot, in principle, be challenged. Justice is what God commanded. As Ashari, the noted Islamic theologian, observed, God's justice is beyond human categories and thus does not restrict His acting with the human as He wishes. Indeed, God rules by fiat, thus reducing justice to his power, reducing right to might.

12. But of course, devoiding the human of free will necessarily implicates devoiding him/her of accountability and thus of responsibility and this certainly presents a serious drawback to the viability of the religious enterprise (certainly in the formulations under consideration here). As such, it should not be surprising to encounter in many of the philosophic and theological explications of Islam various attempts to find a *modus vivendi* that would both retain God's omnipotence and at the same time arrogate to the human some measure of free will (seeing that only some measure but not necessarily unbounded free will are required in order to safeguard the accountability and responsibility of the human). Thus, for example, we can encounter the formulation that arrogates to God omnipotence but claims that God chooses to restrain His infinite power, thus providing room for the expression of free will on the part of the human. Or, alternatively, we can encounter in Asharism a modification of the foregoing formulation in that God is alleged to create and thus bring about everything (thus safeguarding God's omnipotence) but He does this in a plurality of possibilities, leaving the choice between these possibilities to the free will of the human. Still, these formulations trying, so to speak, to eat the cake and have it too are not really persuasive, seeing that they present us with an argument *ex machina*, i.e., postulating a state of affairs merely in order to make possible the feasibility of something which we would like to see take place. And in any case, if God restrains His power or allows choice among a plurality of possibilities, His power as regards its applicability in actuality is inescapably compromised—God's omnipotence may perhaps be abstractly retained in theory but not in actual reality.

13. This may seem to be in contradiction with the Islamic claim that the human does not bear the divine image, seeing that negating the possibility of bearing the divine image implies the wholly otherness of God vis-à-vis the human and thus that God's transcendence is qualitative and not merely quantitative. To try and overcome this seeming contradiction we must first start by clarifying our view with respect to the relations that obtain between these notions, i.e., the notion of transcendence, the notion of bearing the image of some other entity and the notion of otherness on the one hand and the two fundamental notions in terms of which reality, in our view, ultimately constitutes itself,

namely the dimension-of-power and the dimension-of-consciousness, on the other hand. Thus, we would want to contend that the notion of transcendence excludes the possibility of implicating both dimensions (i.e., the dimension-of-power, the It-dimension, and the dimension-of-consciousness, the Thou-dimension) in one and the same act. It can implicate only a single dimension, either the It-dimension or the Thou-dimension, with regard to any particular act, seeing that the notion although signifying by its very essence a difference must nonetheless at the same time implicate that the difference be set in the context of one and the same dimension. The two entities involved, entity A, the transcending entity, and entity B, the entity being transcended, must be located in one and the same dimension. There is, strictly speaking, no possibility of an act between entity A and entity B being an act of transcendence if entity A belongs to one dimension and entity B to the other dimension (indeed, in such a situation there can be no act of any kind between the two entities taking place). Indeed, the very signification of the notion of transcendence differs between its usage in the It-dimension, i.e., the dimension-of-power, and its usage in the Thou-dimension, i.e., the dimension-of-consciousness, signifying in the former a going-beyond (seeing that it arises in the context of a continuum implicating, in turn, quantification so that A can transcend B in different degrees from an infinitesimal to an infinite going beyond), and in the latter an over-againstness (seeing that here it arises in the context of a "gap" implicating, in turn, an all-or-none stance rather than the stance of quantification , i.e., gradation). Similarly, the notion of bearing image must implicate that the two entities involved be located in the same dimension. For clearly, an entity constituting itself exclusively in terms of the dimension-of-power cannot bear the image of an entity constituting itself exclusively in terms of the dimension-of-consciousness, and vice versa, an entity constituting itself exclusively in terms of the dimension-of-consciousness cannot bear the image of an entity constituting itself exclusively in terms of the dimension-of-power.

As against the case of the foregoing two notions, however, in the case of the notion of otherness it can be applied either within the context of only one of the two dimensions available to us (as, indeed, is the case with the foregoing two notions) or alternatively within the context of both dimensions. Namely, entity A can be established as other than entity B either when entity A is located in one dimension and entity B is located in the other dimension or when both entity A and entity B are located in one and the same dimension, it being either the dimension-of-power, the It-dimension, or the dimension-of-consciousness, the Thou-dimension. (It should be noted, however, that the otherness in the latter case, i.e., in the case where the otherness is established within the context of a single dimension, constitutes itself differently, depending on whether its constitution takes place within the dimension-of-power or within the dimension-of-consciousness. In the former instance the otherness is constituted on the basis of the gradation in the power possessed by the entities involved—entity A is other and entity B because entity A possesses more or less power than entity B—thus reflecting the continuum and the quantitative differentiation characterizing the dimension-of-power. In the latter case, on the other hand, the otherness is constituted on the basis of the uniqueness of the content of the consciousness possessed by the entities involved—entity A is other than entity B because the content of its consciousness is unique to it as is B's content of consciousness unique to B—thus reflecting the "gap," i.e., the over-againstness, and the qualitative differentiation characterizing the dimension-of-consciousness.)

Now, we would submit that otherness cannot be established as an otherness that is wholly other if both entities involved in the notion of otherness locate themselves in one and the same dimension. They have to locate themselves one in one of the two available dimensions and the other in the other dimension. This is so because for wholly otherness to be established the two entities implicated must differentiate themselves from each other in terms of the most fundamental aspect characterizing their being, and this means that they have to differentiate themselves in terms of their respective ontological constitution. Their respective ontological constitution cannot be in any way whatsoever identical—they must be qualitatively differentiated from each other. And this can be attained only if entity A is located in one dimension and entity B in the other dimension. When entity A and entity B are located in one and the same dimension, they have, in the last analysis, the same ontological constitution, namely, if the common dimension is the dimension-of-power, their ontology constitutes itself in terms of power and if it is the dimension-of-consciousness, their ontology constitutes itself in terms of consciousness. And if this were the case, then, though the two entities are certainly not excluded from being differentiated, their differentiation must be based on secondary, less fundamental aspects of their ontology as, for example, the differentiation with respect to the extent of power possessed respectively by the entities or the differentiation with respect to their respective contents of consciousness. The otherness therefore that can be obtained when entity A and entity B locate themselves in one and the same dimension cannot be an otherness that is wholly other, a wholly otherness—it can only be an otherness that is less than wholly, an unwholly otherness.

Thus, when Islam rejects the possibility of entity A bearing the image of entity B but also claims that entity A is transcended by entity B, our analysis here would lead us to suggest that we are encountering here an inconsistency. For in rejecting the possibility of entity A bearing the image of entity B the wholly otherness of entity B from entity A is necessarily implicated which, in turn, implicates the exclusion of the possibility of transcendence, i.e., the exclusion of the possibility of entity B transcending entity A, seeing that entity B cannot be wholly other than entity A and at the same time, strictly speaking, transcend entity A inasmuch as the notion of transcendence must necessarily implicate some linkage between the two entities implicated in the relation of transcendence, i.e., between entity B and entity A. Thus, one cannot have both transcendence and wholly otherness characterize the relation between two entities. When Islam, therefore, maintains both characterizations with regard to the relation between the human and the divine, it is putting forth a claim that is, strictly speaking, inconsistent. This inconsistency, however can perhaps be accounted for by the following consideration. Namely, Islam rejects the possibility of the human bearing the image of the divine not because of the notion of the wholly otherness of the divine but primarily because of the notion of the infinite transcendence of the divine believing that bearing the image of the divine would necessarily compromise the infinity of the divine's transcendence. In other words, the implication here is that a transcendence that is infinite excludes any possibility that the two entities in the relation could share in common anything between them. It is here that our position differs. For according to our position, a sharing in common of the ontological constitution would not compromise the infinity of the transcendence. On the contrary, such a sharing is required by it. For without such a sharing no transcendence could arise to begin with and as such, of course, no transcendence that is infinite. On the other hand, the notion of wholly otherness could not possibly arise if there were such a sharing in common between the two entities with regard to their respective ontological constitutions. Indeed, the notion of wholly otherness necessarily implicates the abrogation of any sharing with respect to the ontological constitution of the entities involved—it can arise only when such a sharing is excluded. For the notion of wholly otherness signifies a differentiation (to be precise, a total differentiation) that is of a qualitative kind and a qualitative differentiation (be it total or partial) can be established only within a context that implicates otherness in terms of the ontological constitutions of the entities involved. And this is in clear contrast to the notion of transcendence (including a transcendence that is infinite) which signifies a differentiation that is merely of a quantitative kind and therefore always formulates itself within one ontological domain (to be precise, only within the domain of the dimension-of-power, seeing that a quantitative differentiation can be established only within the confines of this dimension).

Lastly, we may note in this connection that the ascription of wholly otherness to the divine entity precipitates a serious problematic for the religious enterprise, seeing that it abrogates any and all communication between the divine entity and the human entity and vice versa between the human entity and the divine entity. Karl Barth, the leading proponent of ascribing wholly otherness to God, tries to overcome this problematic by claiming a one time divine breakthrough into this-worldly time and history through the incarnation of His word in Jesus Christ. But such a claim suffers from two weaknesses. First, it can be asserted only within the context of faith and not within the context of reason; and secondly, the possibility of communication that it opens up relates only to the communication from the divine to the human but not to the communication from the human to the divine. Indeed, Barth in his later writing mitigates considerably this claim by introducing the motif of the humanity of God. Indeed, Barth's ascription of wholly otherness to God must be seen in its historical context, namely, as a reaction against Ritschlean theology (in particular against Adolph Harnack) and its humanization of God and His reduction into temporality and history. However, from our vantage point this reaction went to the opposite extreme and as such both positions, that of the Ritschleans and that of the early Barth, are, in the last analysis, unsatisfactory. In liberal theology (e.g., Ritschleans and others) we have, so to speak, a formulation that provides the feasibility of eating the cake but does not provide the cake, while in crisis theology (i.e., Barth and his followers) we have a formulation that provides the cake but does not provide the feasibility of eating it. But for the religious enterprise to be viable both conditions, i.e., having the cake and the feasibility of eating it, must be satisfied and this clearly is not the case in either of these two formulations.

However, it would seem to us that these two conditions could be satisfied in a third formulation which situates itself between the two opposing formulations of liberal and crisis theology, a formulation that could provide us both the cake and the feasibility of eating it. This formulation grounds itself in the perception that the sum total of all entities constituting reality divide themselves into three qualitatively distinct kinds of entities, the entities of nature, the divine entity and the human entity (this perception, by the way, was used very creatively by the Jewish philosopher Franz Ronsenzweig). These entities, we would submit, are qualitatively distinct from each other by virtue of the fact that each possesses a different kind of ontological constitution—the entities of nature constituting themselves exclusively within the context of the dimension-of-power, i.e., as pure It entities, the divine entity constituting itself exclusively within the context of the dimension-of-consciousness, i.e., as a pure Thou entity, and the human entity constituting itself within the context of both the dimension-of-power and the dimension-of-consciousness, i.e., as an It/Thou entity. As such, this formulation would, of course, have to accede to a wholly otherness between the divine and nature (thus negating the validity of the notion of a divine creator of nature). But at the same time, as regard the relation between the human and the divine and, indeed, between the human and nature, while a qualitative ontological differentiation between the entities involved is maintained (after all there is clearly a qualitative ontological differentiation between an entity constituted ontologically as a pure Thou or as a pure It and an entity constituted as an It/Thou), these two relations do not implicate a wholly otherness between the entities constituting them. For the human entity by virtue of the fact that it is ontologically constituted as an It/Thou can on the one hand interact with the divine, seeing that both participate in the same ontological dimension, i.e., the Thou-dimension, and on the other hand interact with nature, seeing that here too both participate in the same ontological dimension, except that here it is the It-dimension. Thus, this formulation provides us with an exclusively personal God, i.e., a pure Thou-God a God who in His ontological constitution is other (though not wholly other) than the human and at the same time retains the feasibility of interaction between Him and the human (an interaction that applies in both directions, to wit, from God to the human, i.e., revelation, and from the human to God, i.e., prayer).

14. By the way, the Kalif is the leader in both the political and the religious domain thus presenting Islam as a theocracy. We encounter a similar theocratic union between the political and the religious domain also in Judaism, though only when it formulated itself in the priestly but not in the prophetic strand and also, needless to say, only when the Jewish nation possessed sovereignty. Thus, in the Hebrew bible, when it expresses itself within the priestly strand the office of kingship seems to have combined itself with the priestly office when the king acted as the high priest in the Temple cult (see the dedication of the Jerusalem Temple by King Solomon or the intimations of the king fulfilling the functions of the high priest in celebrating the coming of the new year) and even more pronouncedly in the time of the Great Assembly when the *Nasi,* i.e., the head of the Assembly, was not only the religious but also the political leader thus being both a religious and a political functionary (this in clear contradistinction to the prophetic strand where there is a very clear separation and distinction between the function and status of the king and that of the prophet). Thus, there is an underlying similarity with respect to the issue of theocracy between Islam and Halachic Judaism when the latter expresses itself within the priestly strand. Clearly, the underlying common denominator here is that both express themselves here within the dimension-of-power. In this connection, it is interesting to note the similar underlying similarity pointed to above between Christianity and Judaism when Judaism formulates itself within the priestly strand and when Christianity formulates itself within the Catholic/Orthodox strand, namely, when it accommodates itself to the pagan religious orientation, characterizing the Roman/Hellenistic world (and again here too the common denominator consists in the fact that, in the last analysis, both expressions ground themselves within the dimension-of-power).

Lastly, we ought to note that the underlying similarity noted here between Islam and Judaism is by no means limited to the aspect of theocracy. Indeed, a case can be made that Islam emulates Judaism (both the Judaism of the Hebrew bible and of Halachic Judaism) with respect to a wide spread of aspects ranging from less fundamental aspects such as, for example, the rites associated with burial, the ritual of circumcision, the observance of the Law devolving on the believer only after the onset of puberty to very fundamental aspects of both religions as, for example, formulating themselves via the Law (the Shari'a in Islam and the Halacha in Halachic Judaism, rather than via speculative doctrines thus both being orthopraxist rather than orthodox in the way they constitute themselves, or in the nature and status of their religious functionaries (the mullas in Islam and the rabbis in Halachic Judaism), they being legal scholars and teachers rather than priests, i.e., people endowed with special sacredness and thus set apart from the ordinary believer and exclusively entrusted with executing the rites of the religion. Indeed, Islam can be seen as the placement of Halachic Judaism within concrete history being as such its missionizing agent, so to speak, to the pagan world. But as such this may also implicate a serious drawback for Islam. For while the formulation characterizing Halachic Judaism works reasonably well in the circumstances of exile existence, i.e., in the circumstances of existing, so to speak, outside history, it is not at all clear that it can work equally well in the circumstances of existing within concrete history particularly in the context of the modern world. If anything any number of weighty considerations would indicate that it cannot. Halachic Judaism is an adaptation to exile existence; when, however, it is introduced into an existence that possesses sovereignty, i.e., into an existence within concrete history, it becomes problematic. And, by the way, this observation impinges not only on Islam but also on Halachic Judaism itself (and as such specifically on the Orthodox community within Judaism) when it situates itself in circumstances in which the Jewish nation has regained sovereignty as, for example, in the re-established state of Israel.

15. An arithmetical monotheism can formulate itself in either the dimension-of-power or in the dimension-of-consciousness, seeing that an arithmetical oneness is necessarily implicated by the notion of ultimacy and that the notion of ultimacy can clearly and indeed is most likely to arise in both dimensions. For, as already noted, an entity that is taken as ultimate can only be arithmetically one. A multiplicity of ultimate entities would necessarily compromise their respective ultimacy. To the extent, therefore, that an ultimate entity arises in both the dimension-of-power and the dimension-of-consciousness, it would be in both dimensions an entity that is arithmetically one. But while in the dimension-of-power the ultimate entity remains impersonal and thus the monotheism that arises in connection with it can signify merely the arithmetical oneness, i.e., the ultimacy, of the divine entity and nothing else, the monotheism that arises within the dimension-of-consciousness signifies that the divine entity, i.e., the ultimate entity, that arises within its context is not only arithmetically one but personal and as such, indeed, is qualified as personal. Consequently, inasmuch as the monotheism in Islam is a monotheism that stresses exclusively the arithmetical oneness of God (it strongly berates the notion of the trinity in Christianity), it is a monotheism that grounds itself in the dimension-of-power and not the dimension-of-consciousness.

16. It is interesting to note in this connection the contrast but also the underlying similarity between Islam and Halachic Judaism regarding the issue of the linkage between the religious and the political/national domain. For in contrast to the stated linkage in Islam between religion and the state we have in Halachic Judaism the establishment of a linkage (indeed of an inextricable linkage) between religion and the nation, i.e., between the religion of Judaism and the Jewish nation.

The fundamental linkage in Halachic Judaism is indeed between religion and the nation. This is not to say that the state and consequently politics do not occupy a significant place within Halachic Judaism, seeing that the most fundamental requirement and/or expression of a nation existing and functioning within concrete history is the possession of sovereignty and this, in turn, is embodied in the possession of statehood. But precisely as such, the place that the notion of statehood and politics occupy within Halachic Judaism is secondary and not primary to the notion of nationhood. This difference between the position of Islam and that of Halachic Judaism is a reflection of the difference in their respective positions with regard to the question of existing within concrete history. Islam when it first arises among the people of Arabia and even more subsequently when it adopts in a most active way the vocation of missionizing the world to Islam comes quite clearly to exist and function within concrete history and its very successful attainments in this respect result in the creation of Islamic states. Thus, the *umma* (i.e., the nation) of Islam when it expresses itself within concrete history realizes itself in the format of the state and thus in politics. Hence, the primary, fundamental linkage between religion and nationhood is translated into a linkage between religion and the state. In the case of Halachic Judaism, on the other hand, the translation of the linkage between religion and nationhood to the linkage between religion and the state is stymied by the fact that the nation loses its state and thus its sovereignty and is driven into exile, there to be dispersed in diaspora existence among various host nations. And although the nation manages to survive in these circumstances by the fact that the viability of its religion is retained (indeed, as we shall see below in greater detail, Halachic Judaism is precisely the religious adaptation that made the retention of the viability of the religion here in the circumstances of exile existence possible), the linkage between religion and the nation which is retained in these circumstances (the retention being dictated by the fact that the religion here by the very essence of its formulation necessarily implicates this linkage between itself and the nation so that the survival of the religion necessarily implicates the survival of the nation) cannot be translated into the linkage between the religion and the state, seeing that the nation has lost here its sovereignty. Indeed, the nation existing here in the circumstances of exile existence cannot and indeed does not exist within concrete history (in the circumstances of exile existence it cannot make, i.e., impinge upon, history, nor can it be changed by history—it can only be the passive recipient of the strokes of history).

Lastly, it may be interesting to note that there seems to be a linkage between formulations that ground themselves in the dimension-of-power and their openness to the adoption of theocracy, namely, to combining religion with politics. In contradistinction, formulations that ground themselves in the dimension-of-consciousness do not have such openness. Thus, for example, the Catholic Church, whose formulation, as we have seen, tended to tilt its grounding towards the dimension-of-power, has maintained a close connection with the state and thus with politics, with the Church constituting itself not only as a religious community but as a state with the pope being not only the highest religious leader but also at the same time the sovereign political leader (indeed, until the latter part of the 19th century a good part of Italy was a papal state and even today the Vatican is not just, so to speak, the headquarters of the Church but a sovereign state). In contrast, Protestantism, tilting its grounding towards the dimension-of-consciousness when breaking away from Catholicism, has distanced religion from politics (a noted exception being Calvinism). The rationale for this discrepancy should not be difficult to fathom. A religious formulation that grounds itself in the dimension-of-power is grounding itself in a dimension in which power is not only not a problem but is the fundamental ingredient characterizing all its transactions and thus would likely be inclined to incorporate into itself a linkage to the state and politics, seeing that the state and politics are manifestations of power. On the other hand, a religious formulation that grounds itself in the dimension-of-consciousness is grounding itself in a dimension whose fundamental ingredient, i.e., consciousness (or in religious terminology, spirit), is clearly distinct from (and we might even say opposed to) the ingredient of power, and this being the case, the state and politics, they being manifestations of power, are either to be rejected or, at best, minimally tolerated (seeing that they provide order and peace). The role of religion with respect to politics in this context is that of criticizing or guiding power, not of dispensing it. It is the role of opposition, not of government. This is nicely exemplified by the role assigned to the prophet in the Hebrew bible.

17. This arrogation of justice as the essential attribute of God in Halachic Judaism is in clear contrast to both Islam and Christianity where the arrogation of the essential attribute to God is infinite power in Islam and agape, i.e., unconditional love, in Christianity, seeing that both of these attributes implicate a grounding in only one of these two dimensions (in the dimension-of-power in Islam and in the dimension-of-consciousness in Christianity) and that as such with respect to both of these religious formulations, i.e., the religious formulation of Islam and that of Christianity, the notion of justice is, in the last analysis, neutralized inasmuch as the notion of justice must implicate a grounding in both dimensions if it is to be meaningfully applicable.

But moreover, even within each one of these two dimensions taken in themselves, justice is neutralized inasmuch as it is overridden by the essential attribute characterizing each of them respectively. Thus, as already noted, in Islam where the essential attribute is power and where indeed the divine is constituted predominantly in terms of power, the attribution of infinite power to God per force empties out the notion of justice of its signification when applied to God's acts, seeing that justice here does not retain an independent status in the light of which God's acts can be evaluated. Indeed, inasmuch as might makes right here, ultimate might necessarily implicates ultimate right which is to say that any act of God is per force *ab initio* a just act. As such the notion of justice here becomes devoid of any, so to speak, cash value. Likewise, a similar situation presents itself within Christianity though the rationale here is in terms of a notion, i.e., the notion of agape, that grounds itself in the dimension-of-consciousness rather than in the dimension-of-power. Namely, inasmuch as the essential attribute arrogated to God here is agape and that agape by its very signification must exclude its submission to any further conditions introduced by any vantage point external to itself, introducing justice into the picture here would necessarily undermine the notion of agape—God's acts cannot be dictated by agape and at the same time submit themselves to the evaluation of justice.

Indeed, as such, God's acts cannot be challenged from the vantage point of justice either in Islam or in Christianity. As seen, Islam is thoroughly fatalistic and in Christianity the watchword is "Thy will be done" (though in Islam the fatalism is with respect to God's running the world, thus with respect to God acting in the context of the dimension-of-power, while in Christianity it is with respect to God's acting in extricating the human from his "flesh," his body, thus acting in the context of the dimension-of-consciousness on behalf of the domain of the spirit against the domain of the material). In sharp contradistinction to this, in Halachic Judaism (and indeed in the Hebrew bible), challenging God's acting is fully acceptable and legitimate. Indeed, from its inception when Abraham challenges God "Is the judge of all the earth not to do justice?" through Job, the aftermath of the Chmelnizki massacres to the Holocaust in our day, Halachic Judaism comes to contain a great many challenges to God's acting. There is no denying that the problem of theodicy has been a most troubling and nagging problematic for Halachic Judaism.

18. The story of creation does not originate, however, in the Hebrew bible; it is, in all probability, adopted from Babylonian mythology. Indeed, as had been pointed out by von Rad, the religious phenomenon that is Judaism does not start with the story of creation (nor, for that matter, with the story of the patriarchs) but with the event of the exodus. Also, it should be noted, that with very few exceptions (for example, in deutero-Isaiah) the theme of creation is hardly mentioned in the Hebrew bible. Lastly, a good case can be made that the religious phenomenon of Judaism (certainly in its prophetic strand) does not stand or fall with the story of creation (extirpating Genesis I from the Hebrew bible and thus doing away with the notion of God as creator would not affect the religious phenomenon that is Judaism).

19. The role of partnership is, however, reduced considerably in Halachic Judaism as compared with its role in the prophetic strand in the Hebrew bible due to the exilic existence implicating the loss of sovereignty in which Halachic Judaism expresses itself and which as such necessarily curtails the extent to which the human could participate in the running of the world.

20. The notion of resurrection, however, should not be identified and thus confused with the notion of afterlife, though the two notions are admittedly close in that both implicate a life after death. They nonetheless are two distinct notions in that the notion of afterlife implicates a life that is not terminated by death but continues beyond it and, indeed, continues unendingly albeit in a different place and perhaps in a different form, while the notion of resurrection implicates a life that is interrupted by death and then at a later point is reinstated for an indeterminate duration. Most significantly, the notion of

afterlife, given its delineation here, implicates an intimate connection to the predicament of the finitude of human existence by presenting itself as the answer that overcomes that predicament, to wit, that death does not really signify the end of human existence. As such, the notion of the afterlife by virtue of its intimate connection to the predicament of the finitude of human existence is a notion that grounds itself in the dimension-of-power, seeing that the notion impinges upon such aspects as the aspect of finitude and that of the endless ongoingness of existence, aspects that implicate quantification and that quantification can arise only within the context of the dimension-of-power. As against this, the notion of resurrection inasmuch as it does not necessarily connect itself to the predicament of finitude or necessarily signifies an unending continuation of existence, namely, inasmuch as it does not necessarily implicate aspects that are quantifiable, is not a notion that can be seen as grounding itself in the dimension-of-power.

21. In Halachic Judaism the notion of afterlife enters the picture on the popular level of folk psychology where the belief in it is indeed very widespread and rather deep. However, in the "official" expression of Halachic Judaism, i.e., in its expression in the classical authoritative sources, the notion of the afterlife does not seem to have played any role which should not be surprising, seeing that the finitude of human life does not seem to constitute itself as the basic predicament for the phenomenon of Judaism (certainly not in its expression in the prophetic strand). The basic predicament for Halachic Judaism in its "official" formulation is that the recompense to the human individual for his/her deeds in this life does not measure up to the requirements of justice by the time death occurs. For if death signifies the absolute end to human life and the recompense meted to the human by that point is the final word, then we are inescapably confronted with the problematic of God being unjust, seeing that given the tenet of providence God is, so to speak, running the show and thus ultimately accountable for the injustice and this is a state of affairs which Judaism (specifically in its prophetic strand) cannot accept. The problematic of theodicy, the challenge of "A righteous person and he suffers, an evil person and he prospers" (Tzadic vera lo, rasha vetov lo) must be overcome and a solution must be put forth whereby it can be established that indeed "God is righteous, there is no evil (injustice) in him" (Ki Yashar Adnoai, veain avlata bo). The solution advanced by Halachic Judaism is to claim that death is not the end of the story; it is not the point where, so to speak, the accounts are finally settled. A point in the future beyond death is posited in which the final settlement of accounts will take place, i.e., the last day of judgment, and there full justice will prevail. It is in this context that the tenet of resurrection, not linked to the tenet of afterlife, comes to play an essential role in Halachic Judaism, seeing that it signifies the reinstatement of the human individual into life at that future point, thus allowing him/her to participate in the last day of judgment and thus receive his/her just recompense.

22. It would no doubt have been noted that the various considerations here with respect to the three "daughter religions" focus in the main on two categories in their structure of faith, namely, the category of the divine and the category of worship. The rationale, and indeed justification, for this lies in the fact that these categories are fundamental to the structure of faith of the three "daughter religions" (as indeed they are to all religions) and as such they are as good a compass as any to give us the orientation of these religions and thus establishing the dimension in which their grounding takes place. Namely, having considerations regarding the divine or worship that ground themselves in the dimension-of-power or alternatively in the dimension-of-consciousness is a very good indication that the structure of faith as a whole of the religion in question is one that grounds itself in the dimension-of-power or in the dimension-of-consciousness.

It should perhaps also be pointed out that whether our grounding of any specific consideration is to be in the dimension-of-power or in the dimension-of-consciousness is by and large determined by us on the basis of three criteria: 1) is God a person or an impersonal being (for example, a blind power), 2) is the "gap" between the human and the divine preserved or is it abrogated being supplanted by a continuum, and 3) is the relation between the human and the divine a two-way relation of affirmation or is it a one-way relation of utilization, the former alternatives in all three criteria implicating a grounding in the dimension-of-consciousness while the latter alternatives implicate a grounding in the dimension-of-power.

23. The loss of power and sovereignty by the Jewish people to foreign empires, i.e., to the Seleucid and subsequently to the Roman Empire, elicited three different reactions within the Jewish people. There was the reaction of the Zealots who turned to power to fight back the foreign intrusions. Secondly, as against this, there was the reaction of the Essenes and early Christians who withdrew from the world of power to a spiritual realm. And thirdly, as we shall presently see below, there was the reaction of what became Halachic Judaism which retained itself within a this-worldly context by adapting Judaism to the new situation where power and sovereignty were no longer available.

24. This is clearly manifested, for example, in the fact that all their various divine entities express and manifest themselves in terms of nature. Even more fundamentally it is manifested in the fact that the structure of all pagan religions is inextricably linked to the dimension-of-power and that the dimension-of-power expresses and manifests itself exclusively within the domain of nature, nature being the only domain available to our experience in which the dimension-of-power can be encountered.

25. Of course, a good case can be made that there were other factors that enabled the Jewish people to survive in exile-existence. Thus, for example, the conditions of existence which the Jewish community, by and large, managed to maintain in exile-existence, what has been referred to as the establishment of "a state within a state," thus allowing the Jewish community a significant degree of autonomy in running its own life; or the fact that its exile-existence was at the same time also a diaspora-existence, i.e., an existence dispersed among many host-nations, thus greatly reducing the chance of simultaneously subjecting the nation in its totality to persecution and expulsion—persecutions and expulsions were inflicted in different places at different times thus allowing the rest of the nation to survive when the existence of the persecuted segment was placed in grave jeopardy. Still, the essential and, in the last analysis, defining factor was the feasibility of the religious formulation adopted by Halachic Judaism from the biblical prophetic strand to survive in exile-existence.

26. Of course, once the grounding in the priestly strand is retained, other elements from the priestly strand and thus from the dimension-of-power beside the ritualistic law could and did enter Halachic Judaism such as the rise of a mystical tradition, the preservation of the sacredness of old sites or the introduction of new sacred sites. But these expressions are, in the last analysis, peripheral and not defining for Halachic Judaism.

IV

The Religious Phenomenon in the Context of the Modern World

Before bringing this survey to a close, we should venture to see, albeit very briefly, what impact the rise of the *Zeitgeist* of modernity in the Western world since the 17th century and its subsequent intrusion in recent time into large parts of Asia and the Middle East may implicate for these various concrete historical manifestations of the religious phenomenon.[1] There can be no question, it would seem to us, that the secularist orientation characterizing the *Zeitgeist* of modernity is here to stay and, indeed, to continue growing, and we maintain this notwithstanding the fact that in recent years there has been a pronounced turning back to a traditionalist, ritualistic formulation in practically all of the living religious communities, certainly in the three "daughter religions" with which we are here most directly concerned. We do not see it, however, as signifying a permanent turning back to the traditionalist formulation. Rather, we see it as a temporary backlash against the onslaught of the *Zeitgeist* of modernity. And if this be the case, then the phenomenon of religion is confronted with a serious challenge by the *Zeitgeist* of modernity.

The confrontation can manifest itself on two distinct levels. On the first and most basic level (though the second level is very serious in its own way) it can manifest itself in challenging the very *Weltanschauung*, i.e., world-orientation, which every concrete historical expression of the religious phenomenon implicates, seeing that the *Zeitgeist* of modernity in its secularist orientation clearly contains a *Weltanschauung* of its own which may basically agree with the *Weltanschauung* of the particular concrete historical religious expression or may radically differ from it. On the second level it can manifest itself in challenging not the substance, i.e., the content of the *Weltanschauung* of the particular concrete historical religious expression, but rather the format through which it formulates and expresses this content. Thus, for example, it may well challenge the mythical format of a formulation (specifically, when it is taken literally) that accepts the reality of supernatural entities and their miraculous interventions within the world of ordinary sense-perception. And as such, of course, the confrontation on this level may encompass also a challenge to the way of life, i.e., the customs, mentality, conduct that constitute the ethos of the particular community, and though the ethos is not, strictly speaking, part of the structure of the religious phenomenon it is nonetheless greatly indebted to the religious phenomenon, seeing that it is intimately linked to it.

Now, using the foregoing two possible forms of confrontation we can perhaps stick our neck out and make a few sweeping generalized claims regarding the challenges which the *Zeitgeist* of modernity may or may not present to the various major concrete historical expressions of the religious phenomenon, to wit, pagan religion, Islam, Christianity and Halachic Judaism. Thus, to start with the religion of paganism, it would seem to us that in principle there is no real conflict on the first level, i.e., the level referring to the content of the *Weltanschauung*. For after all, in the last analysis, both *Weltanschauungen* ground themselves squarely within the dimension-of-power. The only difference between these two *Weltanschauungen* on this level is ultimately in terms of the degree regarding the possession of reliable knowledge with respect to how power works and the degree regarding the ability to manipulate and utilize the workings of power. Indeed, it is this difference in degree that leads to a confrontation on the second level, i.e., the level of the format of expression. Here, the two *Weltanschauungen*, that of pagan religion and that of the secularism characterizing the modern world, may very well clash and this, in turn, would express itself in the clash between the magical/miraculous and the empirical/rational approach as manifested respectively in the mythical and scientific formats of expression. Thus, the confrontation between the pagan religion and the *Zeitgeist* of the modern world would basically clash on the second but not on the first level, i.e., on the level of the format of expression but not on the level of the content of the *Weltanschauung*.

And this assessment would also apply in our view to the next expression of the religious phenomenon, i.e., to Islam, except that here the conflict would be more pronounced. This is in a way to be expected, seeing that Islam, even though with respect to the content of its formulation, by virtue of its tilting its grounding towards the dimension-of-power, comes to share to a considerable extent the same grounding as pagan religion, its grounding within the dimension-of-power is nonetheless, in contrast to that of pagan religion, mitigated by the fact that it, unlike pagan religion, also maintains a grounding in the dimension-of-consciousness and as such this would clearly precipitate a more pronounced clash with the grounding in the dimension-of-power that characterizes the *Zeitgeist* of the modern world. Still, this clash is not nearly as pronounced as the clash implicated in the confrontation that takes place on the level of the format of expression. The antagonism and opposition of Islam to the *Zeitgeist* of the modern world seems to be primarily not on the level of content but on the level of the format of expression. It is the undermining by the *Zeitgeist* of the modern world of the mythical and miraculous way of grasping our world and of the traditional ethos characterizing the life of the community that causes and propels the virulent reaction of Islam to the *Zeitgeist* of the modern world.[2] But beyond this there is the further consideration that would account for the fact that the reaction of Islam to the *Zeitgeist* of the modern world is so much more pronounced than the reaction of pagan religion. This consideration lies in the fact that in contrast to pagan religion, which formulates itself in terms of the plurality of the pantheonic gods, which as such are merely penultimate entities, Islam formulates itself in terms of an arithmetical monotheism that implicates that it formulates itself in terms of a divine entity that is an ultimate entity. As such, this means that the confrontation here with the *Zeitgeist* of the modern world is from the vantage point of an ultimate entity and not from the vantage point of penultimate entities which, in turn, would mean that the mitigation and compromise that a religious expression formulating itself in terms of penultimate divine entities (e.g., pagan religion) could sustain, could not be tolerated by a religious expression that formulates itself in terms of an ultimate divine entity (e.g., Islam) thus making the clash with an alternative *Weltanschauung* much more pronounced and unyielding.

In moving to the third expression of the religious phenomenon, i.e., to Christianity, we encounter, in contradistinction to pagan religion and to Islam, an expression in which the confrontation with the *Zeitgeist* of the modern world manifests itself primarily on the first level, i.e., the level of the content of the *Weltanschauung*, and not on the second level, i.e., the level of the format of expression. And here on this level of the content of the *Weltanschauung*, the confrontation would express itself in a fundamental clash, seeing that the expression of Christianity cited here tilts its grounding in considerable measure towards the dimension-of-consciousness while the *Zeitgeist* of the modern world grounds itself firmly in the dimension-of-power. Of course, as such the Christianity cited here is the Christianity that expressed itself in the Nazarene sect (it being a forerunner to Christianity proper), in Paul (to some extent), in some of its portrayal in the New Testament, in the different hermetic and monastic communities, in various expressions within Reformation Protestantism and in our time in such movements as the Evangelical and Pentecostal movements. At the same time, however, inasmuch as there are, as we have already noted, expressions within Christianity that shift the pronounced grounding within the dimension-of-consciousness back towards a more noticeable grounding within the dimension-of-power (such expressions that can be encountered, for example, in the Catholic/Orthodox strand) the clash with the *Zeitgeist* of the modern world on the level of content would be commensurately also mitigated.

Coming lastly to the fourth expression of the religious phenomenon in our series, the expression of Halachic Judaism, it would seem to us that inasmuch as Halachic Judaism strives to properly balance its grounding between the dimension-of-consciousness and the dimension-of-power this balancing would reflect itself in its confrontation with the *Zeitgeist* of the modern world thus keeping the clash with the *Zeitgeist* of the modern world on a more restrained and mitigated level whether it takes place on the level of the content of the *Weltanschauung* involved or on the level of the format of expression. As such, indeed, Halachic Judaism would find itself again in a midpoint position between the position of Islam and that of Christianity. It may clash with modern science but only if a few of its writings are to be taken literally (for example, the story of creation in Genesis). In terms of its essential formulation, however, it can accept modern science (for example, the "big bang" theory or the theory of evolution) without really undermining in any significant way its essential content and message. Likewise, there can certainly be a clash between it and the *Zeitgeist* of the modern world if a number of the ways in which it chose to express itself (for example the narration of miracles, the intervention of angels) are to be taken at face value. But such ways of expression are relatively few (which, by the way, should not be surprising, seeing that under the impact of the ethical monotheism originating in the prophetic strand in the Hebrew Bible and being fully incorporated within Halachic Judaism, mythological and miraculous expressions were by and large eradicated or considerably mitigated). Thus, the clash between Halachic Judaism and the *Zeitgeist* of modernity on both the level of content and that of expression is relatively muted.

But this is by no means to say that the rise of the *Zeitgeist* of the modern world has had no significant, indeed profound and fundamental, impact on Halachic Judaism. It most certainly did. But the impact was not derived directly from the confrontation with the *Zeitgeist* of the modern world either on the level of content or on the level of expression. Rather its derivation is mediated through a manifestation, albeit a central manifestation, of the *Zeitgeist* of the modern world, namely, the phenomenon of the Enlightenment, which in turn brings about the emancipation of the Jewish people in their exile-existence.[3] Now, the Enlightenment both directly and through the mediation of the phenomenon of the Emancipation impacts most seriously and fundamentally the feasibility of the survival of the Jewish people in exile-existence. Through its direct impact it undermines the prospects of the ritual law continuing to be operative. For the Enlightenment, seeing that it grounds itself exclusively in reason, fails to find an acceptable rationale or justification for an enlightened person to observe the dictates of the ritual law (thus, for example, what acceptable rationale would there be fore observing the dietary laws or the laws pertaining to the observance of the Sabbath and the holidays), particularly seeing that their observance interferes with and counter-acts the assimilationist trends induced by the Emancipation (thus making the Emancipation an important contributing factor here). But this being the case, it means that the religious expression that defines Halachic Judaism can no longer be operative for, as we have seen, the ritual law provided the content for the religious vocation that characterizes the religious expression defining Halachic Judaism and without a vocation the religious expression is doomed to die. But with the religious expression characterizing Halachic Judaism becoming inoperative, the very essence and *raison d'être* of Halachic Judaism is abrogated which, in turn, means that the feasibility of the survival in exile-existence of the Jewish people qua being Jewish becomes highly dubious, seeing that the very existence of the Jewish people in retaining its distinctiveness as being Jewish is inextricably linked to an existence of the religion of Judaism that is viable and operative and that the expression of this religion that has proved itself adaptable to exile-existence is the religious expression characterizing Halachic Judaism. Thus, if the religious expression characterizing Halachic Judaism becomes inoperative, then the prospect for the survival of the Jewish people qua being Jewish in exile-existence becomes untenable.

The prospect for the survival of the Jewish people qua being Jewish in exile-existence becomes even more dubious under the impact of the Emancipation which is implicated by the Enlightenment. The Emancipation meant in essence the opening up, so to speak, by the host nation of its gates and allowing the Jews to enter, participate and partake in its life. It meant doing away with a "ghettoized existence" for the Jews and removing the disabilities and restrictions that went along with it. The Emancipation certainly offered the Jews many advantages and benefits. But these offerings affected the Jews qua human beings but not qua Jews.[4] Indeed with respect to the Jews qua Jews the Emancipation gave rise to two trends which seriously threatened the survival of the Jewish people in exile-existence, they being the trend towards assimilation on the part of the Jews and the trend towards embracing modern anti-Semitism on the part of the host nation, both implicating, in the last analysis, the extinction of the Jewish people qua Jewish except that in the former case it was to be attained through a kiss of death while in the latter case it was to be attained ultimately through physical extermination.

Thus, as regards the trend towards assimilation, it is built into the very process of the Emancipation. For as already noted, the instigators of the Emancipation expected and indeed made it a condition for the Jew to leave his/her Jewishness behind—the Jew was to be accepted as a human being but not as a Jew. But moreover and more importantly, the very process of the Emancipation by including the Jew within the life of the host nation inescapably implicated his/her being drawn into the culture, the ethos of the host nation (not to mention that the Jew once emancipated was most desirous and anxious to immerse him/herself in the culture and the ethos of the host nation). As such, the emancipated Jew was destined to, sooner or later, lose his/her Jewish heritage and disappear as a Jew (though not necessarily as a human being). And as regards the other trend, namely, the trend towards modern anti-Semitism, it in essence is a continuation of the age-old manifestation of anti-Jewishness, seeing that in both manifestations the fundamental factor that brings forth these manifestations is the foreignness, the otherness of the Jew when he/she is situated within the host nation.[5]

There is however an all-important difference between modern anti-Semitism and the preceding anti-Jewishness in that while in the latter case the factor of foreignness, otherness, expressed itself mainly in terms of the religious difference, in the former case, under the impact of the rise of nationalism in modern Europe, it expresses itself mainly in terms of the ethnic/national difference (thus in a way justifying the application of the new name of anti-Semitism even though it is, strictly speaking, much too broad and thus inaccurate). The Emancipation, however, greatly exacerbates this difference between the Jews and the host nation in bringing the Jews into the life of the host nation and thus making them that much more visible (and to the extent that the Jews are used as a scapegoat, their participation in the life of the host nation provides them more readily as a scapegoat). At the same time, however, the reaction of the host nation, when reflecting the sentiments of modern anti-Semitism, towards the foreignness and otherness of the Jews, remains basically the same as that of the preceding anti-Jewishness. Namely, the reaction in both instances expresses itself in the imposition of discriminating policies, persecutions, exclusion and expulsion, except that given the considerably increased power which is now placed at the disposal of the host nation, due to the great advances in science and technology, the manifestations of these expressions can be, and very often are, much more virulent.[6] Thus, the prospects of survival for the Jewish people in exile-existence within the context of the Emancipation are very problematic, if not indeed very dim. But if the Jewish people qua Jewish cannot survive in exile-existence within the context of the Emancipation, then Halachic Judaism likewise cannot survive, seeing that it becomes irrelevant inasmuch as it no longer has a community to address. Indeed, by the same token that the Jewish people qua Jewish cannot survive without the religion of Judaism, the religion of Judaism cannot survive without the survival of the Jewish people. And since we are dealing here with the survival of the Jewish people in exile-existence within the context of the Emancipation, the religion of Judaism that could apply here could only be the religion of Judaism when it formulates itself as Halachic Judaism.[7] But, as we have tried to show the formulation of Halachic Judaism is undermined by the secularism characterizing the *Zeitgeist* of the modern world precisely with respect to the aspect that enabled it to be operative and thus relevant in the context of exile-existence, i.e., with respect to its adoption of the ritual law. And in addition to this it is further undermined by an implication of the *Zeitgeist* of the modern world, i.e., by the process of the emancipation of the Jews, which precipitates a serious threat to the survival of the Jewish people qua Jewish in exile-existence and which as such would deprive Halachic Judaism of the community it requires in order to be operative and thus relevant. In terms of either aspect the relevancy of Halachic Judaism for the Emancipated Jew is seriously undermined.

So, in bringing this survey to a close, let us underline again that our reflections here are intended exclusively to ascertain and assess the factors that may have a bearing on the outcome of the confrontation between the secularist *Zeitgeist* of the modern world on the one hand, and the Pagan and Biblical religions on the other. It in no way presumes to prophecy, i.e., predict, the nature of the outcome. This belongs to the future and is not available to us. Indeed, there is a rabbinic saying which states that since prophecy ceased in Israel (i.e., after the last three biblical prophets Haggai, Zachariah, and Malachi) anyone who claims to be a prophet is either a fool or a knave. Not wishing to be either, we better stop here and say no more.

Notes

1. The essential feature of this *Zeitgeist* lies in its secularist orientation, i.e., an orientation that constitutes itself exclusively in terms of a this-worldly, horizontal perspective and totally excludes an other-worldly, perpendicular perspective. This secularist orientation, in turn, expresses itself in a variety of ways such as the materialist, the empiricist and the rationalist modes of perception and thinking, modes of perception and thinking that exclude the mythical, other-worldly perspective. Thus, for example, magic is excluded and replaced with scientific/technological manipulations and miracles are likewise excluded and replaced with scientific/rational explanations. Clearly the secularist orientation remains firmly grounded within the context of the dimension-of-power.

2. Indeed, this manifests itself in the contemporary situations in the fact that this reaction of Islam finds its most forceful expression, by and large, among those segments of the Islamic population that are, so to speak, less sophisticated and critical in their thinking. Indeed when Islam expressed itself through more sophisticated and critical minds as, for example, was the case between the 11th and 14th centuries C.E., its response to the secularist orientation was quite different. Islam was leading the way in embracing the secularist orientation that grounded itself in the dimension-of-power as was manifested, for example, in its full embrace of Greek philosophy and the science of that day.

3. The process of emancipation does not take place all at once in all the countries of Jewish dispersion and on all levels of human life such as the economic, the educational, the political and the social. Rather its progression is gradual moving geographically over approximately a hundred and fifty years from its inception in Western Europe to Eastern Europe and finally when the Jewish populations in Islamic countries are driven to settle mainly in Israel (with some settling in various Western European countries) and at the same time progressing in stages from the economic to the educational to the political and finally (and still only partially) to the social level.

4. Indeed, they were offered to the Jews as human beings and not as Jews. The original advocates and promoters of Emancipation who, interestingly enough though not really surprisingly, came not from the Jewish side but from the side of the host nation representing the liberal wing and closely associating themselves with and being motivated by the orientation of the Enlightenment, took as their slogan "to the Jew as a human being everything, to the Jew as Jew nothing." Though the motivation in resorting to this slogan may well have been to counteract the fears and objections of the conservative/reactionary camp, the slogan captures a valid aspect of the Emancipation.

5. There is an additional factor that plays a role here and needs to be mentioned in passing though it is not as fundamental as the factor of the foreignness and otherness of the Jew. This additional factor is constituted by the lack of physical power by the Jewish people in exile-existence (and perhaps even more so by the absence in their ethos of the drive to resort to whatever physical power they did possess) and their small numerical presence which as such made them a very convenient scapegoat on which to place the blame for every failure and dissatisfaction that the host nation may incur.

6. The observations made here are, we would submit, poignantly exemplified in the policies of the Nazis towards the Jews who came under their control so that the Nazi's

atrocious acts vis-à-vis the Jews can be taken as the expression, albeit in an exaggerated form, of the tendencies implicated in the orientation of modern anti-Semitism. Thus, they impose discriminatory policies (e.g. the Nürenberg laws), pursue forceful exclusion (e.g., incarceration in concentration camps), organize and encourage the physical molestation and the killing of Jews and the burning and destruction of their synagogues and businesses (e.g., Crystal Nacht) and finally their adoption of the slogan *Judenrein* (i.e., free of Jews) to articulate the goal to which they were striving. Indeed, until the outbreak of World War II, Jews who could get visas and thus emigrate out of Germany to other countries were allowed and indeed welcomed to do so (the real tragedy here was that so many countries including, sadly to note, the United States were rather reluctant to accept the Jews). It was with the outbreak of World War II which by and large closed the possibilities of emigrating or escaping German domination and the expansion of German domination over most of Europe (and most significantly, given our concern here, over Eastern Europe, seeing that the bulk of the Jewish population lived in that part of Europe) that in the absence of the possibility of expulsion and given the pathological blind hatred of the Jews just for being Jewish that the devilish idea of, so to speak, expelling the Jews by physical extermination arises leading to the gas chambers of the concentration camps.

7. For that matter, it may be noted that the survival of Halachic Judaism could not really be salvaged in the solutions that were advanced in response to the problematic precipitated by the Emancipation. There were, in the main, two solutions: that of political Zionism which addressed the problematic when it expressed itself in terms of the rise of modern anti-Semitism and that of cultural Zionism which addressed the problematic when it expressed itself in terms of the loss by the people of their Jewish heritage resulting from the trend towards assimilation induced by the Emancipation. The solution which cultural Zionism suggested was to secure a critical mass, i.e., a large enough size, of the Jewish population in any particular location which as such could safeguard and, indeed, nourish the development of Jewish culture. To the extent, however, that the locations of such centers would be in the diaspora thus in exile-existence, this solution advanced by cultural Zionism suffers from a serious flaw. For the safeguarding and nourishing of Jewish culture requires not only a critical mass of the Jewish presence but, equally important, a considerable degree of autonomy and distance from competing cultures, conditions that are very unlikely to be met in exile-existence. The Bundists in Poland were apparently cognizant of this as they indeed proposed a form of Jewish autonomous self-rule in exile-existence. The problem here is that in all likelihood the host nation would not accept such arrangements, not to mention the many practical difficulties in actually constituting such a plan (and indeed the Bundist's plan did not take).

The only location where this solution could be realized would have to be a reinstated Jewish homeland which means that the solution advanced by cultural Zionism must presuppose the realization of the solution advanced by political Zionism, namely, the need to regain a homeland which would give the Jewish people their own sovereignty which, in turn, means the incorporation of cultural Zionism within political Zionism. But in the context of a regained homeland and being in the possession of one's own sovereignty, the expression of the religion of Judaism in the formulation of Halachic Judaism is no longer by any means the necessary formulation nor, for that matter, the best formulation. Indeed, the best formulation in this context, seeing that it alone can represent in an uncompromised way the distinctiveness of the religion of Judaism, would be the formulation that grounds itself exclusively in the prophetic strand excluding the sharing of this grounding with an additional partial grounding in the priestly strand (i.e., the state of affairs that characterizes the formulation of Halachic Judaism). In other words, it would be the formulation in which the religious vocation would be viewed from the vantage point of a social ethics and not of a ritual law.

www.ingramcontent.com/pod-product-compliance
Lightning Source LLC
Chambersburg PA
CBHW021133300426
44113CB00006B/412